Toledo's Three Ls

LAMSON'S, THE LION STORE & LASALLE'S

BRUCE ALLEN KOPYTEK

THE
History
PRESS

Published by The History Press
Charleston, SC 29403
www.historypress.net

First published 2013

Manufactured in the United States

ISBN 978.1.60949.758.3

Library of Congress CIP data applied for.

To the late Sylvania Franciscans Sister Mary Leontius Zawistowski and Sister Mary Marcelline Drewniak, superlative educators and the dearest of friends.

"As Toledo Grew, So Grew Lasalle & Koch's." A 1936 ad for the store that was "more than a store, a community institution." *Collection of the author.*

Contents

Preface   7

Acknowledgements   11

Introduction: A Tale of Two Cities   13

Pride of Place   21

Toledo Born—Toledo Owned—Toledo Operated   43

The New Lamson Store   50

Toledo's Own Store   60

What's in a Name?   74

There's No Place Like Home   83

Lion Tales   94

Toledo's Greatest Store   105

More Than a Store, a Community Institution   113

The Larger Lasalle & Koch Store   128

Branches in the Great Black Swamp   140

Nothing Good Lasts Forever   160

Appendix A: Store Locations   177

Appendix B: Store Directories   181

Bibliography   189

About the Author   191

Preface

It seems a bit incongruous, but exploring the history of three long-gone department stores has proven to be a revelatory and exasperating experience at the same time. It is especially so when subject matter necessary to the very task itself has been difficult to uncover. In a number of cases, famous defunct stores have left behind preserved archives, which hold valuable photographs, business information and a treasure-trove of history. Gimbels, B. Altman & Company, Woodward & Lothrop and Chicago's revered Marshall Field & Company are just a few "dead retailers" whose chronicles have been preserved in one way or another. Often, these archives were donated to local museums, libraries and universities. Others, such as Michigan's Jacobson's, had their archives saved from the trash heap by a single employee who was bent on keeping an institution's legacy alive.

Not so the Three *L*s that are the subject of this book. Though their histories make more than worthwhile study matter and their achievements were beyond notable, their day-to-day records, photographs of their interiors and historical notes do not seem to have been preserved en masse at any location. Aside from a few artifacts here and there, the very means that could illuminate just what these stores were and how they became a part of their hometown are very thin on the ground.

Word of mouth thus becomes a great factor in the uncovering of what could be named "forgotten history." The oral histories of people who either worked for or patronized Lamson's, Lasalle's and the Lion Store reveal a

Aerial view of 1940s Toledo. The subject department stores are highlighted and noted by name. *By permission of the Toledo-Lucas County Library.*

living and tangible link to the stores' histories and the deeper meaning and subsequent understanding of their existences.

On the other hand, the pursuit of personal memories is likewise not an easy task, especially given the years that have gone by since these well-known marques left the Toledo scene. Lamson's, for the most part, closed almost forty years ago, meaning that many of the store's older employees have since passed away; anyone who was younger at the time of the store's demise either doesn't remember much or is perhaps not a fully participating member of today's "social network" society. As a result, Facebook, blog and website postings requesting information have mostly gone unnoticed by them. Lasalle's and the Lion Store lasted longer, to varying degrees, and it might be thought that photos and information about the stores could still be found at the large corporations who inherited a few of the stores; but these entities, who themselves are struggling through difficult economic times, are mostly unwilling to answer a request regarding any material of historic interest in their possession.

From this situation emerges a salient question: How can the history of the Three *L*s be exposed, illuminated and put back together for the wider public to enjoy? In addition to the verbal, and occasionally written, accounts mentioned above, the task of uncovering these histories is made a bit easier by the fact that the stores themselves were a part of the social media of their day: local and national newspapers. Department stores were prolific advertisers, and as a result, the papers themselves covered their activities and events quite extensively.

A drawback of this coverage is that it forces the memory of department stores, which became anchors in their communities and an active part of their customers' lives, through a filter that renders all output in black and white, be it printed word, drawing or photograph. Still, just as small fish can fit through a fisherman's net, this filter has allowed something of the stores' vivid operations and admirable environments to sneak through and illuminate the subject matter.

So the verbal, written and illustrated material on hand can be examined along with artifacts held in a variety of Toledo institutions to compose a history that could begin to stir the imagination of and evoke a sense of nostalgia in potential readers' minds. That is the purpose of this book.

Once this purpose has been achieved, however, a veil is lifted, and the discovery, the revelation and the sheer interest of what emerges warrant further investigation in this journey of discovery. New questions arise whose answers must be pursued: What was society like in a time when the mere building of a new department store in a city like Toledo elicited page after page of newspaper comment and advertising? How did these stores draw customers to one downtown location, enlivening the areas in which they conducted business and creating a remarkable commercial and cultural center which itself has passed away? Who were their founders? What made them so individual, and who were their employees? As well, who were their customers, and what role did the Three *L*s play in their lives?

All these things can yet be gleaned from information that still exists, albeit in many places and buried quite effectively, given the ravages of time. What emerges is invariably interesting, illustrative and worthwhile but elicits sadness too. A reader of *Jacobson's, I Miss It So!* told me:

> *I loved reading the book. I feel as if I got to know the characters and the places where all this history took place. But when it came to the chapters that covered the demise of the store and how the employees and customers responded, I felt as if I were in a state of mourning myself, that I should be in a funeral parlor, signing the guest book and reminiscing about someone dear who had been lost.*

It is no different with the Toledo stores. For years longer than a typical human lifetime, they existed in the epicenter of a place with its own related history and bore witness—through owners, employees and customers—to the changing fortunes, joys and sorrows of a unique time and place. No understanding of Toledo could be complete without an insight into what the Three *L*s were to people who knew them.

Having understood the locale, the discernment of the history portrayed in this book then breaks open a wider question. Toledo, home to the Three *L*s, was once the third-biggest city in Ohio, an industrial powerhouse and home to immigrants who came to it in order to find the proverbial "better life." If department stores played a role in this phenomenon, how many other cities of vaguely similar size—the Fort Waynes, the Oaklands or the Rochesters—witnessed similar events?

Furthermore, if the Toledo of today doesn't resemble the setting that was home to these department stores, what happened? Why should it be so different? If the department stores represented an honorable and valuable part of the city's makeup, what, if anything, has replaced them, and why do we settle for anything less than what they represented?

It is in considering these questions that this journey of discovery transcends a mere "department-store history." It takes a deeper look into the life and times of a particular slice of civilization, in this case the city of Toledo, Ohio, and how the subject matter—namely the Lamson Brothers Company, the Lion Store and the Lasalle & Koch Company— took their places in the larger story. The reader is invited to share in this exploration and appreciate how these stores' chronicles played a role in a truly extraordinary culture. The stores and the world they inhabited are sadly only a memory today.

Acknowledgements

S orry to say, not much that is easily accessible remains of Toledo's Three *L*s to produce a work worthy of their history and importance. I have relied on many individuals and am deeply thankful that they so willingly and generously offered assistance in uncovering a history worth telling. Donna Christian of the Toledo–Lucas County Public Library went well out of her way to assist me. Jamie Farr proved his reputation as the very antithesis of a Hollywood star by being accessible, kind and overflowing with memories of his time spent in Toledo and these stores. A special thanks is due to Judd Silverman for helping me contact Jamie; without that simple act, huge chunks, very human ones, would be missing from this book. At the University of Toledo's Canaday Center, Arjun Sabharwal was especially helpful in fulfilling research on the topic at hand. I am also deeply thankful to those individuals who answered my requests for memories and artifacts, including Abbot Justin DuVall, Sarah Hogoboom, Brent Bissell, Nancy Pihlaja, Diana Dunsmore, Stephany Anderson and Sheila Book. Scott Nimmo provided images of credit cards from the Three *L*s, and I also thank an anonymous Toledo donor for a Lion Store artifact. By far, the most difficult of the stores to research was Lamson's because it disappeared so long ago; Wendy Towle and her mother, Catherine Towle, were generous with their time and archival materials, which were indeed a game changer for the book. Their help would not have been possible without the work of Lawrence Stine, of the Historic Old West End Toledo website, who advertised my search for material on his charming and information-packed pages. Many thanks to John McCleary for relating his memories all the way from Arizona.

Furthermore, I am grateful to my brother, Patrick Kopytek, for support and his company on many trips to Toledo and its environs, and to my niece Dr. Rachel Klamo for her advice and calming influence when I truly believed that I was not up to the task. Looking back into my past, I have nothing but admiration and respect for the Sylvania Franciscan Nuns for providing me with a Toledo connection, which began when I was in seventh grade at Our Lady of Good Counsel School in Detroit, and also for Toledo's Stranahan Foundation, which, through my parents' work at the Champion Spark Plug Company plant in Detroit, granted me a merit scholarship years ago that financed a good part of my education at the University of Detroit.

Saving the best for last, I am forever indebted to my sweet wife, Carole, who has sacrificed so much to be the kind and generous partner she is; I could produce nothing without her help, loving support and influence, as they say, "in good times and in bad."

Introduction
A Tale of Two Cities

Before settlers populated an area of northwestern Ohio, there was a place named Toledo. Before the founding of Lamson's, the Lion Store or Lasalle's, there was a marvelous city named Toledo. In fact, before there ever was a department store at all, there was Toledo, and its history went back a long time before that as well.

Rising above the Río Tajo (Tagus River in English), like the shining biblical "city on a hill" first elucidated in Christ's Sermon on the Mount, Toledo was ensconced like a jewel in the midst of the arid windmill-dotted landscape of La Mancha in Spain and was an oasis of art, faith, politics and, in fact, all things that composed city life. After the Romans, who called the city Toletum, were usurped by the Visigoths, Toledo seemed to sway with the winds of time. After three hundred years as the refined capital of the Visigothic Empire, it fell to the Moorish conquest, becoming the Caliphate of Córdoba's launch pad to further Muslim conquest of the Iberian Peninsula.

No longer a capital, Toledo under Moorish control eventually became a center of rebellion against Córdoba, until the whole caliphate disintegrated into a series of semi-independent principalities, or taifas. These taifas, of which there were many, competed with each other for prestige and thus sought to attract the best writers and artists as a source of enrichment. Toledo was the center of one of the greatest taifas, but like the rest, it was militarily weak. A particular characteristic of Toledo was the coexistence

Panorama of Toledo, Spain, from one of the cigarrales across the Río Tajo (Tagus). *Photo by the author.*

within it of the three great monotheistic religions, a fact alone that enriched its cultural landscape.

Meanwhile, about 250 miles to the north, the Asturian king Pelayo defeated the advancing Moors, thereby launching the seven-century-long Reconquista, the Christian reconquest of the Iberian Peninsula. Pelayo's burial place in the sacred cave of Covadonga in the dramatic Picos de Europa mountain range of northern Spain remains a destination for pilgrims to this day and commemorates the start of the Reconquista in the year 722.

Almost four hundred years later, the Castillian king Alfonso VI, "El Bravo," conquered Toledo in the midst of a squabble with his four siblings, who were each granted a portion of the Christian Spanish Kingdom of their father, Ferdinand I of Castile. Toledo eventually became the capital of Alfonso VI's kingdom and entered into a great period of cultural and artistic advancement.

The significance of this period in Toledo's history lies in the translation of Arabic literature by Jewish and Christian scholars, thereby disseminating knowledge and long-lost information into an ascendant Europe, which was emerging from the Dark Ages and hungry for them both. Toledo flourished as a center of art and culture until the Spanish court moved, ultimately to Madrid. The following decline, while it robbed Toledo of prominence, preserved its history and its treasures intact. The era of tolerance ended at the dawn of the sixteenth century, when the remaining Jews and Muslims were either converted or expelled. Their legacy, in the stones of the old city remained, however, as many mosques and synagogues were converted into churches. The *Mudéjar* style of architecture found throughout Toledo refers to medieval, gothic or renaissance designs that have been embellished with elements of Islamic design in brick and plasterwork, reflecting a symbiosis of the two cultures.

Toledo's treasures are housed in a city of resplendent beauty and abundant life. Seen from one of the *cigarrales* (country estates) across the Tajo, it appears as a sea of small tile-roofed houses, surmounted by the dual highlights of the great royal palace of the Alcazar and the majestic cathedral punctuating its brilliant skyline. Spanish historian and author José Domingo Delgado Bedmar, describing the historical and cultural phenomenon that is Toledo, writes:

> *Few Spanish cities have given rise to as much literature as Toledo. Thousands of pages that have attempted to explain that mysterious and inapprehensible something the city provokes and which, throughout time, has fascinated and engaged the traveler. However, the more we write about Toledo, its art or its history, the more we become aware of the existence of a thousand and one subtleties, a thousand and one suggestions, a thousand and one details that are difficult to put down in words.*

The delights of Toledo take many forms, from the small scale and common place in the form of its famous marzipan or the unique damascene jewelry sold in its shops to the large scale and monumental, such as its lively Plaza de Zocodover, where all the city seems to congregate. The loftiest and most enduring of the city's jewels is its awe-inspiring cathedral, described by Toledo author Rufino Miranda as a monument that "makes a person feel proud to belong to humankind…everything that faith, art, and history can offer have been stored up here, until it is now filled to the brim with a collection unique in its diversity and impressive in its opulence."

The church, which lies at the spiritual heart of Spain, receives its designation as cathedral due to being the seat of the Primate of all Spain. The sanctuary, like the city it inhabits, is a composition of layers, artistic and cultural, which have been built up over time. As such, it is a combination of styles, from pure gothic with its soaring heights and sublime light filtered through stained glass to Mudéjar and Plateresque, the latter being another Spanish style in which stone is worked into elaborate designs "as if by a silversmith." Among the distinguished cathedral's *embarras de richesses*, two stand out. The first, known as the Transparente, is a glorious Baroque altarpiece of marble, jasper and bronze bathed in light from above. The other is the enormous painting of the *Disrobing of Christ* by the Spanish Renaissance artist El Greco, which hangs among Titians, Goyas and Van Dycks in the cathedral's sacristy.

El Greco, the Crete-born artist who came to Toledo and stayed for the last thirty-seven years of his life, created the greatest of his masterpieces in his capacious studio within the walls of the city. The dark, expressionist canvasses populated by tortured, elongated figures presaged the twentieth-century expressionist movement by hundreds of years but was, in fact, a reflection of the artist's early training as an icon painter in his native Greece.

One of his greatest triumphs, the *Burial of the Conde de Orgaz* hangs in El Greco's parish church of Santo Tomé, a few blocks from the cathedral. It portrays a legend from the fifteenth century in which Saints Stephen and Augustine themselves were said to come down to earth from heaven to officiate at the burial of a just, pious and righteous nobleman who had endowed the small neighborhood church in his will. The large radiant painting indeed portrays the coming together of heaven and earth, but the townspeople and noblemen assisting in the burial and surrounding the body of the dead knight are in fact portraits of well-known Toledoans of the artist's day. The members of the aristocracy who esteemed the artist and paid for his work were thus immortalized on canvas as well.

These aspects, and many, many more, of the city of Toledo serve, in combination, to illustrate just what it is that makes it a great and noble city. It is the variety, the richness and the mixture of these traditions, monuments and artworks with the day-to-day life of the city that make it, not a museum of things past, but a living, breathing organism, composed of an incomparable wealth and vibrant with life as a result. It is no wonder that the city is a constant draw to tourists and art lovers as well. Needless to say, it has been hailed as a World Heritage Site by the United Nations Educational, Scientific and Cultural Organization (UNESCO).

Toledo, Ohio, built up in the nineteenth century on a swamp where the mouth of the Maumee River empties into Lake Erie, shares a lot with its namesake in La Mancha. How they came to have the same name is something of a mystery, but several versions of how it came to pass were summarized in an advertisement published by the Lasalle & Koch Company around the hundredth anniversary of the founding of the city. Two adjacent townships, Port Lawrence and Vistula, chose to combine to improve their chances to be selected as the northern terminus of the Miami and Erie Canal, which was begun in 1825 to connect the Ohio River at Cincinnati to Lake Erie.

Owing to rivalry between the two factions, it was decided to give the combined town a new name. Several individuals have taken credit for the result, but most of their stories have been disproven by one fact of history or another. The Lasalle & Koch ad of 1937 gives credence to the version that an early Port Lawrence merchant named Willard Daniels suggested "Toledo" at a meeting of the various personalities involved because of his having read the history of the old Spanish capital and the fact that there was at the time no other town in North America bearing the same name.

If the above account is true, it can be seen as quite prophetic. Toledo, Ohio, like its namesake, became a city of education, industry and art. Like other mid-sized American cities, the qualities of Toledo attracted people, creating wealth and fueling growth. It is not possible to understand the history of the Three Ls without examining the why and wherefore of the city which grew up on the banks of the Maumee River.

Incidentally, the canal that would have seemed to be the raison d'être for Toledo's existence became obsolete not long after it was completed due to the rise of railroads and their inevitable march across North America. The new mode of transportation turned out to be a great benefit to Toledo. It was located at the intersection of a major north–south line from Detroit to Cincinnati and a major east–west route that connected New York and Chicago via Cleveland, a distinct strategic advantage for a city looking to attract industry and wealth.

Hard-working Irish immigrants settled in the city to work on the railroads as they flourished. With the resultant industrialization that characterized Toledo, other ethnic groups came to settle on the banks of the Maumee as well. Toledo's population nearly quadrupled ten years after its founding, and by the 1870s, when the first waterworks were installed, the population had swelled to almost thirty-two thousand people. With them came schools, a library, an opera house and other civic amenities increasingly geared to a city on the move. A good example was the most elegant hotel of the day, which stood on the corner of Madison and St. Clair Streets: the Boody House (a name which would probably never to be applied to a hotel today), named for Azariah Boody, head of the Wabash Railroad.

In 1868, Toledo was promoted in a pamphlet issued by promoter and real estate magnate Jesup W. Scott as the "Future Great City of the World," quite an indicator of the optimism of the age. That faith played a role in the life of Toledo from an early age is demonstrated by the presence of Presbyterian, Episcopalian and Methodist churches in Port Lawrence and Vistula while Lutherans and Baptists came later. Father (later bishop) Amadeus Rappe came to the city and established its first Catholic church in 1841. Catholic church spires and bell towers appeared increasingly on the fledgling city's skyline, as new parishes were formed to serve Toledo's Irish, French and German communities.

Toledo also promoted itself as an ideal location for industry. One of the first and most enduring fruits of this proactive search for capital was the relocation of the Libbey Glass works in Toledo from Massachusetts in 1888. While the Libbey's start-up was rocky to say the least and profits were initially hard to come by, the firm's last-ditch effort to promote its products with a stunning exhibit at the 1893 World's Columbian Exposition in Chicago caused a sensation and created far-ranging demand for Libbey's products. It was by Libbey's presence that Toledo soon acquired the popular moniker of the "Glass City," but before the turn of the century, other industrialists, among them Michael Owens and Edward Ford, had arrived as well, following Libbey's example.

Another famous name in the Toledo manufacturing world of the day was Dr. Allen DeVilbiss, who developed modern spray-painting technology, and his son Allen Jr., who invented the springless measuring scale and sold his patents to what would become the Toledo Scale Company, whose products were once found in practically any meat, produce or fish market in the country. After the turn of the century, brothers Frank and Robert Stranahan moved their Champion Spark Plug manufacturing company to Toledo in order to be near the Willys-Overland auto manufacturing plant, which was second only to Dearborn's Ford Motor Company in car production leading up to World War I.

The population swelled at the time to over two hundred thousand people, over 20 percent of them foreign-born immigrants ready to work in the city's factories. The great majority of these people were from Poland and Hungary, though sizable Russian, German and Middle Eastern communities swelled the city as it grew. These people invested what they could of their income to build neighborhood churches that they could call their own; as a result, landmarks such as St. Hedwig's and St. Stephen's came to serve the faith needs of the Polish and Hungarian enclaves in the city.

Soon, streetcar lines crisscrossed Toledo to transport people from their homes to their jobs and to the downtown, which was rapidly developing as a service and entertainment center, from the retail-oriented Summit Street parallel to the Maumee River westward to the Beaux-Arts Lucas County Courthouse, which had been built in 1893 to serve as the nucleus of a developing government center. Madison Avenue took on the role of Toledo's business and financial district and was the home to Toledo's first skyscraper, the 1892 Nasby Building, which was designed as an adaptation of the world famous Giralda Tower located in Seville, Spain.

To be of service to residents and their families, various religious organizations found a home in Toledo. The city had a YMCA from its earliest days. In 1854, a congregation of Ursuline nuns arrived in Toledo from Cleveland and

Skyline of Toledo, Ohio, in the 1940s. The riverfront is given over to industrial uses, but behind the buildings lies a vibrant urban center. From a postcard. *Collection of the author.*

ministered to the population while developing a private educational system from scratch. Later, the Sylvania Franciscan Nuns came from Rochester, Minnesota, in order to be of service to the city's growing Polish-born population. Under the dynamic leadership of Mother Mary Adelaide Sandusky, the order became innovators in the fields of education and healthcare. Originally headquartered at St. Hedwig Parish, they acquired land in 1917 in outlying Sylvania, where they built a beautiful Spanish mission–style convent that continues to flourish. The nuns' familiar brown habits (cream colored in warmer seasons) were a familiar site in the Toledo covered by this book.

Toledo attracted the attention of the fine-art world when its Museum of Art was incorporated in 1901, at which time it occupied temporary quarters, until it opened the doors to its present Greek Revival–style building on land donated by Edward D. Libbey. Later, Libbey donated the funds for its expansion, which included two symmetrical wings that were completed in the late 1920s. One of the wings housed the unique Peristyle Hall, a performing arts venue that has been the scene of great performances not only by the Toledo Symphony Orchestra but also by soloists and ensembles from around the world. The permanent art collection, along with its focus on the art of glass, makes the museum among the most unique and valuable on the North American continent. The seeds of these true splendors in the city of Toledo were sown by the success of the industrialization, growth and prosperity that were as much a part of it as its venerable name.

Neighborhoods were platted, and houses and apartment buildings were built to create communities while parks provided green space for residents. Recreation possibilities included Wallbridge Park with its zoo and amusement park, as well as resort areas to the east along the Lake Erie coastline, accessible by streetcar. Yet Toledo's epicenter was the developing downtown district, with its various dry goods establishments along Summit Street, fine metropolitan hotels, theaters, government buildings, restaurants and office buildings of all sorts. This downtown area developed, grew and became ever more popular despite wars, epidemics, strikes and even the Great Depression. The permanence and integrity of the young city that matured to become Toledo was remarkable.

Even during times of trouble, Toledo was able to build something new. The great Cathedral of Our Lady, Queen of the Holy Rosary, was begun in the midst of the Depression and, when finished, revealed splendors to the city's faithful that were derived from the its namesake overseas. During the WPA era, Toledo inaugurated a new library, whose unique feature was an interior clad, with great élan, in Vitrolite, or pigmented structural glass. The unique building material, common in the art deco era but comparatively rare now, was a gift of Libbey-Owens-Ford to the library, and in this installation, it was uniquely crafted into a series of murals that ring the library's lobby. The glass display, along with the walls, pilasters and columns sheathed in the glass material, blurs the boundaries between construction and sheer, exuberant art.

It would be too easy to find contradictions in a comparison between the two Toledos described here. For instance, from the onset, it is clear that one is a "city on a hill" while the other is a city literally built up from a swamp. But a closer, more detailed and more sincere comparison shows that the contradictions are minor ones. Both cities developed from nothing into worthwhile settlements that attracted the best and brightest of people, and the work of their inhabitants became famous, attractive and desirable. The two Toledos have their place in the world of art, and both have a history that is compelling.

Our Toledo, worthy holder of the name of its predecessor, is where the story of the Three Ls played out. If the city at large—its people, its industry and its streets that spread out and conquered a swamp—is the macroenvironment of the story, the action itself took place in a district of human vitality set amid architectural beauty, the downtown, which demands to be understood as the commercial setting for the history of its three greatest department stores.

Pride of Place

To understand our Three *L*s, we must place them in a setting. For the same reason that a person doesn't carry precious gems in his pocket or hidden in a purse, these department stores are best understood in the context of their place in Toledo's downtown, where they were meant to be seen. The Three *L*s didn't exist on isolated blocks, apart from the teeming life that could be found in the downtown of their heyday. They formed one element of a variety of ingredients, which together brought to life the center of town and made it an attractive place to do business.

Downtown Toledo was not only a retail district. Nor was it just an area in which business offices and churches were located in isolation. It was not just a governmental center, or solely the place where people could find a hotel for the night. It was all of these things, and all of them simultaneously. It housed Toledo's best stores, its most prestigious office buildings, its finest theaters and its greatest hotels within its boundaries or on its fringes, and it housed them cheek by jowl in an area that was easily accessed by the city's population. It was where everything happened, and it was *the* place to be when Toledoans needed to shop, sought entertainment or desired civic participation, not to mention that an enormous daytime population came there to work as well.

The combination worked so beautifully that, until postwar suburbanization began to alter the central business district's status, no one could conceive of shopping, going to the theater or transacting most types of business without thinking of downtown. As such, it was central to not just city but also the lives of most Toledoans.

Jamie Farr, the actor who regularly brought laughter and smiles to the faces of millions of Americans as Corporal Maxwell Q. Klinger on the beloved television series *M•A•S•H*, grew up in the Glass City and, throughout his career—which later encompassed movies, television appearances and critical successes in live theater—has remained a son of Toledo. He grew up on the north side, in a mixed Middle Eastern, Jewish and Polish neighborhood in the vicinity of Mulberry Street. Yet Jamie Farr, who was born into a Lebanese family as Jameel Farah, was no stranger to Downtown Toledo and to this day waxes lyrical when speaking about time he spent downtown:

From the time I was young, I loved movies. And I loved department stores, ever since I was a child. As a kid, I'd go downtown with my mom and her lady friends. We could take a bus right from our neighborhood, see a movie, have lunch and shop, which was a lot of fun in those days, even if we couldn't afford to buy. Just experiencing the displays and the atmosphere of the stores was great. There was so much excitement and imagination in the air. We'd visit all the department stores, and you couldn't go home without sitting on the lions on Summit street or visiting Tiedtke's, which I liken to a "baby Costco" of the day. Everyone loved to go there. They had everything—including the world's largest wheel of cheese—from tires, fruits and vegetables to a huge coffee grinder, which would make a noise that could be heard throughout the store when it operated. Another favorite was B.R. Baker's. It was the best men's store in Toledo, and it was far out of our reach; but once, I was able to find a double-breasted suit for twenty-nine dollars, and boy, that was really something!

Jamie Farr's memories of his youth in Toledo offer an insight into the understanding of this place and its *genius loci*. It combined a great many things that could be experienced at once or in pieces. A favored definition of poetry is "that thing which, if one word is added, or taken away, loses its perfection." Downtown Toledo could be described in a similar way. It had a recipe for success—a combination of hotels, stores, office and professional buildings, churches, entertainment venues and government service buildings, which together added up to more than the parts alone. These parts, importantly, were built not just to house space for activity but also to be the best and most impressive of their kind.

Toledo's older Boody House hotel eventually gave way to several large metropolitan hostelries, which both hosted guests and entertained Toledoans looking for a night out in their lavish dining rooms and show venues. The

Jamie Farr, who, in spite of an acclaimed career in film, television and the stage, still says, "I have wonderful memories of growing up in my favorite city, Toledo!" *Photo courtesy Jamie Farr.*

first of these, located on the southeast corner of Superior and Jefferson Streets, was the neo-Georgian Secor Hotel, which opened in 1908. The detailed brick pile that housed the hotel proper was noted for its lavish interiors and, later, its Candlelight Room was a favored "dinner and dancing" destination. The Secor Hotel was a revelation in its day, offering previously unheard of comfort, and eventually was joined to an art deco garage with first-floor storefronts to its south.

Across the street, in 1927, rose the great, partially executed bulk of Toledo's biggest hotel, the five-hundred-room Commodore Perry. Designed in a more sober, neoclassical commercial style, the third of the three wings that were planned to rise from its four-story base was never built, likely owing to the Depression, but the hotel became arguably Toledo's most famous and popular. Its bar was decorated in Vitrolite panels and was as modern as a prewar German ocean liner. The Travertine Room and later the Shalimar Room restaurants were preeminent destinations for a night of dining and dancing. The Commodore Perry had it all.

Hospitality could also be found at the large 1916 Waldorf Hotel on the east side of Summit Street at Madison Street and at the Fort Meigs Hotel, built around the same time as the Commodore Perry but on a much smaller scale. The Willard Hotel, whose building on St. Clair Street also housed the Valentine Theater, was an example of an older and more intimate hotel that, nonetheless, remained popular for many years. A number of residential hotels were also located in the fashionable residential district just to the west of downtown, namely the Hillcrest and Park Lane.

Three of the great representative metropolitan hotels of Toledo, *from left to right*, the Waldorf, the Secor and the Commodore Perry. From postcards. *Collection of the author.*

All of these places were establishments of great character that served Toledo's hospitality needs admirably and blended with downtown's theaters, stores and office buildings to create an urban and lively environment.

Toledo's government center was the only component of the downtown district that could be described as somewhat isolated. State and federal facilities were generally concentrated near the monumental Beaux-Arts architecture of the Lucas County Courthouse. In fact, the area to the north of the courthouse was planned as a civic center before the Great Depression. A new post office and federal building joined the courthouse in a harmonizing style, and in 1927, when artist Arthur Covey was invited to Toledo to create window murals for the Lasalle & Koch Company, he went out of his way to praise the city's new Safety Building on the Civic Center Mall, calling it, along with the Lasalle & Koch store and the Ohio Second National Bank Building on Summit Street, "the most splendid achievements of Toledo." The Safety Building served as a de facto city hall until the 1980s.

During the Depression, Toledo replaced its old library with a streamlined, art deco edifice across from the courthouse. While modern in design, the building materials related to the monumental structures around it, and its overall character was in affable accord with its neighbors. The library's function added to the variety of services that distinguished Downtown Toledo.

Most of Toledo's theaters were located on St. Clair Street, and that thoroughfare took on the character of a miniature Broadway for the city. The Rivoli and Palace Theaters were located on the east side of St. Clair Street, just north of Adams, while the large Pantheon was to the south, directly across from the Lion Store. The Valentine Theater, often referred to as Loews Valentine, was directly across the street from the Rivoli and the Palace. A few theaters, like the Loop and the Royal, were located nearby on Superior Street. The art deco Loews Esquire was among the newest and largest of Toledo's movie houses, located away from its established rivals but just a block north of the Commodore Perry Hotel.

Most of these movie palaces did more than entertain via the shows and films they presented. Their fantasy style of architecture added to the experience, and at a time when most Toledoans went to the theater to get away from the monotony of everyday life, the lavishness and over-the-top atmosphere on display was like icing on the cake. Often, their street façades barely hinted at the splendors within. One notable exception was Burt's Theater on the corner of Jefferson and Ontario Streets, which looked for all the world like a Gothic palazzo transported to Toledo from the Grand Canal in Venice.

Toledo's burlesque houses were located in the theater district itself or nearby. One of the largest was the Town Hall Burlesque Theatre, which began life as the Capitol Theater. As Toledo's "skid row" developed around the intersection of Summit and Cherry Streets, the theater found itself too close to the area, which was full of run-down flophouses, bars and pawn shops by the 1960s. A former dancer, who had performed at Minsky's famous burlesque theater in New York, decided to settle in Toledo and rechristened it the Town Hall. That her name was Rose La Rose (born Rose DePella) is not all that unusual when, in an era that saw burlesque transform from innocent fun to a risqué form of entertainment, other dancers who appeared in her theater went by names such as "Ann Arbor" "Candy Barr" and "Adoria Derriere." Another burlesque theater was the Gayety, which was located behind a small storefront on Summit Street almost directly across from the Lion Store.

The great office buildings that outfitted Toledo with an upward-reaching skyline in the twentieth century added density to the city and populated the downtown district with workers, who sought the services provided by the area's stores and restaurants. The first example of a taller office building was the National Union Building of 1891, followed a few years later by the previously mentioned Nasby Building. The National Union was replaced by

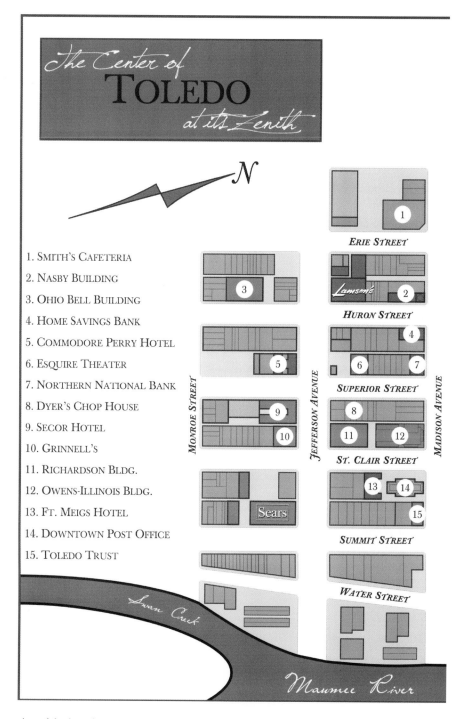

The Center of TOLEDO at its Zenith

1. SMITH'S CAFETERIA
2. NASBY BUILDING
3. OHIO BELL BUILDING
4. HOME SAVINGS BANK
5. COMMODORE PERRY HOTEL
6. ESQUIRE THEATER
7. NORTHERN NATIONAL BANK
8. DYER'S CHOP HOUSE
9. SECOR HOTEL
10. GRINNELL'S
11. RICHARDSON BLDG.
12. OWENS-ILLINOIS BLDG.
13. FT. MEIGS HOTEL
14. DOWNTOWN POST OFFICE
15. TOLEDO TRUST

Artwork by the author.

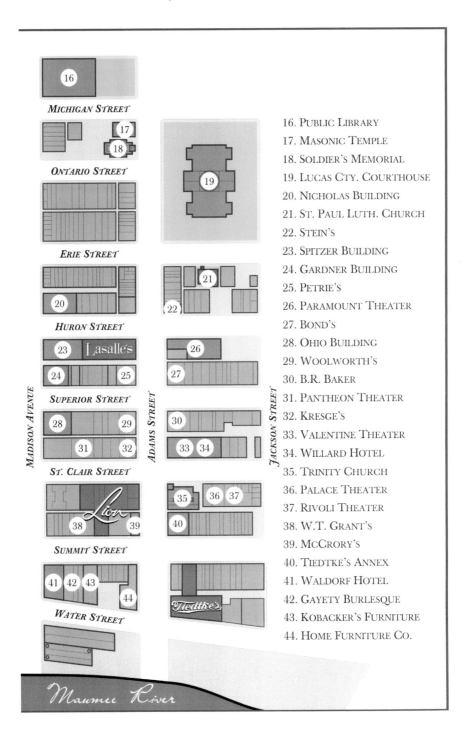

16. PUBLIC LIBRARY
17. MASONIC TEMPLE
18. SOLDIER'S MEMORIAL
19. LUCAS CTY. COURTHOUSE
20. NICHOLAS BUILDING
21. ST. PAUL LUTH. CHURCH
22. STEIN'S
23. SPITZER BUILDING
24. GARDNER BUILDING
25. PETRIE'S
26. PARAMOUNT THEATER
27. BOND'S
28. OHIO BUILDING
29. WOOLWORTH'S
30. B.R. BAKER
31. PANTHEON THEATER
32. KRESGE'S
33. VALENTINE THEATER
34. WILLARD HOTEL
35. TRINITY CHURCH
36. PALACE THEATER
37. RIVOLI THEATER
38. W.T. GRANT'S
39. MCCRORY'S
40. TIEDTKE'S ANNEX
41. WALDORF HOTEL
42. GAYETY BURLESQUE
43. KOBACKER'S FURNITURE
44. HOME FURNITURE CO.

Lasalle & Koch's 1917 store, but the Nasby Building's tower went on to set the tone for Madison Avenue as Toledo's Wall Street, giving it a canyonlike appearance as it acquired more and more finance-related buildings. Among them was the six-story Gardner Building of 1893, a faithful reproduction of a Florentine palazzo.

The revolutionary Spitzer Building also served to reinforce Madison Avenue's unique nature and was technically Toledo's first true skyscraper. It was one of the first to include a public amenity in its layout, namely, an arcade lined with shops that bisected the building and provided an indoor passage from Madison Avenue to Huron Street and later, in conjunction with the Lasalle & Koch Company, all the way north to Adams. The Spitzer Building itself was a prime example of early Chicago-style commercial architecture, beautifully articulated with bay windows that more efficiently brought light to the interior and a liberal use of masonry arches, particularly at the structure's entrances. It was successful enough in its day to be expanded in 1900.

After the turn of the century, Toledo's drive for tall buildings, especially on Madison Avenue, increased dramatically. The Spitzers built the substantial Nicholas Building at seventeen stories, and later the twelve-story Ohio Savings Bank and Trust Building joined it, as did the Home Bank & Trust Company Building, which topped out at ten stories. An exception on the other (south) side of Madison Avenue was the Greek temple–like Northern National Bank Building, which consisted of only two floors—the first dedicated to retail shops at street level, the second to a cavernous banking hall.

The tallest building, by far, in early twentieth-century Toledo was the Second National Bank Building, which climbed a narrow twenty-two stories over Summit Street on the corner of Madison Avenue. Most of Summit Street was decidedly low rise at the time, so the sheer height of the building was emphasized by its environment, especially on its west side, where the old 1888 federal building remained in use as the city's downtown post office.

All these buildings were, more or less, products of the historicism that characterized the work of the best architects of the day. As such, they all bore a generosity of detail that allowed them to transcend their bigness and added to the city streets aesthetically as a result, not to mention their interiors, which, at least in public areas, matched or, in most cases, exceeded the richness enjoyed by passersby outside.

As the 1920s came to an end, architects began to react to artistic movements in Europe and designed buildings in a more contemporary style that still used traditional forms but that was often decorated using geometric or floral motifs. Toledo acquired both a magnificent example of art deco and its tallest building for many years when the new Ohio Bank Building opened on the site of the old Boody House hotel. Thrusting upward twenty-eight stories, the giant building had an impressive vertical emphasis that was softened by its stepped design, which related well to neighboring low-rise buildings, especially owing to the fact that its four-story base served as a podium from which the whole composition soared dramatically upward. Unfortunately, the bank that built it succumbed to the Great Depression, but Owens-Illinois Glass Company bought the building and occupied it for many years.

Most of these components of Toledo's downtown had retail space at the ground level, which further enlivened the streetscape and contributed to the multilayered nature of a downtown district at its best. Summit Street developed as an area identified with retail business, and as the Three Ls grew and moved away from the established retail zone, the streets paralleling the Maumee River gained prominence as locations for stores. Adams Street, which ran perpendicular from Summit Street westbound across St. Clair, Superior and Huron Streets, in essence became a new and fashionable retail corridor. The mix of stores, workplaces, service firms and hospitality venues that composed the downtown was conveniently connected by the crisscross grid of streets, and each had its own character.

The main retail anchor of the southern end of Summit Street was W.L. Milner & Company, which arrived on the scene well after the Three Ls had established themselves on Summit Street. William L. Milner came to Toledo at the age of twenty-two from his native Hartford, Kansas, in 1890. He took a position at the early dry goods business of W.C. McElroy on Summit Street, where he quickly became a partner; later, he took control of the business, renaming it W.L. Milner & Company and relocating it to the 1892 Coghlin Building at Summit and Jefferson Streets. The store proved so popular under Milner's leadership that it was enlarged in 1903 and again in 1906, by which time it became the biggest and most complete department store in Toledo.

Milner's Summit Street premises occupied a lavish six-story building that was also home to Toledo's first escalator. The store placed daily flamboyant full-page ads in Toledo newspapers announcing the day's bargains and events that drew customers to it. Milner's was, at the time, noted as the largest department store between Cleveland and Chicago. The *Toledo Times* in 1903 extolled the virtues of the store's "light, beautiful and perfectly equipped restaurant" on the top floor, adjacent to an auditorium christened by Milner as the "Theaterette."

Lively Summit Street looking south, just north of Adams Street. By this time, Tiedtke's (left) had replaced its ornate marquee with a streamlined version faced in stainless steel. *From a postcard, collection of the author.*

Milner's business success was so great that his name spread beyond Toledo to Detroit in 1908, though in the process, it had tragic consequences for Milner, his family and his Toledo store. The Pardridge and Blackwell department store of Detroit, founded some seven years earlier, had failed and was acquired by one of its biggest wholesale suppliers, the Crowley brothers. Joseph L Crowley, president of the company, asked his Toledo friend William L. Milner to join with him and his brothers to begin a new retail enterprise—Crowley, Milner & Company—where Pardridge and Blackwell left off. In 1909, the new firm commenced business under its new name while Detroit was likewise in a period of dramatic industrial expansion, due primarily to the growth of automobile manufacturing. Within eight years, the store, which had already added two additional floors atop its original structure, filled out a whole city block with its exquisite terra cotta–clad building, also the first in its city to install escalators for vertical conveyance.

In 1921, Crowley's built a ten-story annex that was eventually connected to the main store by a five-level bridge embellished with sizable clocks at the third-floor level on both of its sides. One year later, however, disaster struck. Returning from one of his frequent commutes to Detroit, Milner swerved

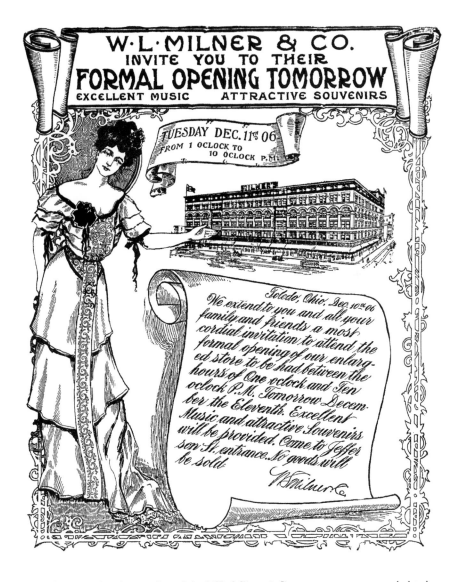

1906 ad announcing the opening of the W.L. Milner & Company store as expanded to its ultimate size. *Collection of the author.*

to avoid an oncoming car while passing a truck on the Dixie Highway at LaSalle, Michigan. His Stutz automobile went out of control and rolled into a ditch, pinning Milner and crushing his chest. The retail magnate suffered for almost two weeks before he passed away from his injuries on September 2, 1922.

The Toledo Milner store continued in business, reorganized under remaining managers and family members, but it would never achieve lasting success, likely due to the absence of W.L. Milner's genius as a businessman. The store tried to reinvent itself as the "New Milner's," but it was all for naught. By the spring of 1928, it was announced that the store would be closed and studies were being undertaken to turn it into a parking garage. A great liquidation sale was the final event at the store that had once seemed to attract all Toledo as it went from success to success.

Fifty-eight miles to the north, Crowley, Milner & Company fared much better, growing to become Detroit's second-favorite department store after the J.L. Hudson Company, and in spite of the loss of its one-time partner and president from Toledo, it kept "Milner" as part of its name for the rest of its effective life. In Toledo, the proposal to convert the Milner Building to parking came to naught, and Sears, Roebuck & Company brought its chain store to Toledo by opening its largest branch at the time in Milner's former building at 143 Summit Street.

An article in the *Toledo News-Bee* about the demise of Milner's speculated about the reasons for the lack of success at its location on the southern end of Summit Street:

> *Trade continued to shift north on Summit Street and west on Adams Street and in a few years the Milner store suffered from a type of isolation that cannot be foreseen or prevented, but can easily be analyzed after it has taken place. The Milner store was caught in much the same manner that some of the largest stores of the country have been hit when, for some unexplainable reason, the retail section of a city starts a rapid shift to another neighborhood.*

The success of the downtown Sears store in the building Milner built seems to give the lie to this explanation; it is more likely that the store struggled by lack of the sort of creative leadership provided by Milner himself. Furthermore, with Milner's death, Toledo lost a true civic statesman who, at one time, headed the chamber of commerce and diligently worked on plans for the city's streetcar system.

In the 1950s and 1960s, small businesses served downtown between the major anchor stores. Across Summit Street from Sears was a variety of small businesses, such as Sanders Pet Shop, Deprisco Music, Gross Electrical Supply, Acme Paints and Mootz Candy Company. The block once housing these businesses is presently known as Fort Industry Square. Continuing north on Summit Street, the block north of Sears, from Jefferson Street to Madison Avenue, likewise sported small shops in older buildings, among them Meeker's Pet Shop, a Glidden Paint Store and Stone's Luncheonette. The Toledo Trust Tower, originally the second National Bank, anchored the southwest corner of the block.

Across the street, Toledo's smaller, secondary furniture stores held sway. Most of the block was concentrated with stores like Johnson Brothers, Kennedy's, Usher's and the Modern Furniture Company, but the corner at Madison Avenue across Summit Street from the Toledo Trust Tower was held down by Hertz's Snack Bar.

The west side of Summit Street's three hundred block was unique in Toledo. It held the main stores of the Three Ls until 1900, when Lasalle & Koch's moved to Jefferson Avenue. In later years, only the Lion Store's annex, with its namesake bronze-plated lions, held sway in the middle of the block. A branch of the S.S. Kresge Company began the block at 301 Summit Street at Madison Avenue, and the storefronts between it and the Lion Store included Lane's Drugs, the Cotton Shop, Field's Hats, Kinney's Shoes and a large W.T. Grant variety store. North of the Lion Store, S.S. Kresge's operated another of its "five and dime" stores at 333 Summit Street, where Lamson Brothers kept shop until 1928. The Carolyn Shops, Dorothy May Fashions and Cole Shoe Store rounded out the block's offerings. Cole's occupied the building once home to Lasalle & Koch's, giving an idea of how big the department stores had grown since their beginnings in the mid- to late 1800s.

Well-known furniture stores dominated the east side of the street between Madison Avenue and Adams Street. The Waldorf Hotel, which vied with the Commodore Perry for title of "Toledo's largest," and its well-known Grill took up the southern end of the block, anchored in the middle by Kobacker's Furniture Store. The Nu Style Chrome Company store and the Gayety Burlesque Theater shared the block between the hotel and Kobacker's, and Paris Jewelers, Thom McAnn's Shoes and the large Basch Jewelry store were some of the businesses between it and its rival, the Home Furniture Company. In later years, the Home Furniture Company, which stood proudly on the corner of Summit and Adams Streets, sported a modern storefront clad with Vitrolite panels.

The block north of Adams was dominated by Tiedtke's, arguably Toledo's most unique retail attraction. Though it had an ornate Georgian Revival façade clad in decorative terra cotta, the bulk of the store was located in a large, plain brick warehouse building to the rear, which stretched along Water Street behind the façades of its smaller Summit Street neighbors. Tiedtke's original flamboyant triple-vaulted marquee was later replaced with a streamlined one that trumpeted the store's name three times in bright red neon letters. Next door, on the corner of Adams and Summit Streets, the old HM&R Shoe Store building housed Mary Jane's and Osterman's Jewelers. On the north side of Tiedtke's, small shoe and furniture stores and even a one-time A&P food market filled out the block to Jackson Street.

Most Toledoans who remember it, such as Jamie Farr, will admit that it was virtually impossible to come downtown without a visit to Tiedtke's just to enjoy its Barnum-and-Bailey atmosphere, have a bite in one of its eating places or pick up a bargain from the vast quantity of foodstuffs and general merchandise on offer.

Its main-floor food departments, the hallmark of the store, were a virtual assault on the senses. Clerks juggled apples and oranges in order to attract attention to them, a peanut-roasting machine hissed and spewed clouds of steam into the air and the giant coffee machine roared as freshly roasted beans slid from a hopper to be ground to order for waiting customers who craved the store's Parkwood roast. An illuminated sign revolved above the giant meat counter, and when the owners realized that the store was indeed a circus, they decided that music should be part of the mix. A phonograph proved unsatisfactory, so a pipe organ was installed; customers could request popular songs of the day, and the instrument belted out the tunes to the clacking of the nearby wooden escalator. Those unwilling to ride it found themselves climbing stairs that had carnival mirrors installed on the landings to the delight of children and adults alike

The aromas of Tiedtke's were so renowned that local businessmen often left their offices saying, "Let's go over to Tiedtke's and smell our lunch!" Inside Tiedtke's doors, a bakery staffed by employees culled from Toledo's many European immigrant communities, a candy department where everything was made in-house, a pipe tobacco shop, a large floral department and a stand-up hot dog and hamburger stand produced the delectable bouquet that permeated the store. In 1950, the *Toledo Blade* quoted a visitor from Boston who said:

> *I never had such an unusual experience as going into this delightful place at holiday time, and hearing the beautiful "Adeste Fidelis" booming out of the*

organ, accompanied by the whistle of the peanut-roaster, and the crash and grind of the coffee machines. There was caviar on one side of me, and cold buttermilk on the other. There was a carnival spirit all over the store, and it was an adventure just to go in this place.

Ernest and Charles Tiedtke were the sons of August Tiedtke, who was born in Marienwerder, Prussia, in 1831 (owing to the shifts of boundaries after World War II, the town is today called Kwidzyn and is located in Poland). According to memoirs left by his granddaughter, August felt uncomfortable in Prussia because he disliked its increasingly militaristic atmosphere, which later reached feverish levels under Emperor Wilhelm II before the Great War. August left and settled in Toledo with his wife, almost by chance, and bought a farm on which they raised their six children.

His son Charles left the farm to seek his fortune in Toledo and, in 1894, asked Ernest, who had relocated to Boston for work, to join him in starting a grocery business. The two brothers were of differing dispositions, but their individual qualities served the business well. Charles was businesslike, introspective and could be most often found wearing a fine suit in his office on the mezzanine, overlooking the store, while Ernest was more of a social creature who wore the same white shop coat that his employees did and spent most of his time on the floor with customers and workers alike. The store was originally known as Tiedtke & Todd, a legend goes, because all prominent businesses had two names, just like Lasalle & Koch. No Todd ever existed as their partner; they just thought the name sounded right in combination with theirs.

The Tiedtkes were proud of their fleet of yellow delivery wagons, drawn by beautifully groomed horses that lived in stables on store property. They also maintained a fishing fleet that brought lake fish to the store fresh every day and even made deliveries out to the many freighters that plied the Great Lakes. It was said that Great Lakes sailors were well known for refusing to go ashore and shop in Detroit, Cleveland or Buffalo when they could visit Tiedtke's while in Toledo.

In many ways, the Tiedtkes were the first to put sizzle and glamor into the retail food business, in a day when food shopping took place in gloomy, unattractive stores. The public flocked to them as a result, and a strong bond grew between the brothers, their employees and their customers. Workers' overwhelming medical bills were, from time to time, paid secretly and mysteriously, and more than once did one of the brothers slip a hundred-dollar bill "across a desk to an employee in trouble, saying, 'Don't tell anyone about this.'" They were also known to quietly host after-hours events for groups of orphans who were allowed to come into the store and select a Christmas present from the enormous selection of toys.

The brothers also hired a protestant minister to serve as store detective. When he would catch a shoplifter, knowing that many of these people were average joes who fell prey to temptation, he would simply take him up to his office and, after giving him a stern look, preach the Gospel to him until he thought the offender was ready to leave.

The store also sold clothing and house furnishings on its upper levels and included a number of restaurants, one of which was a sit-down place, referred to in early ads as "the big restaurant," with a view of the Maumee River. In the early days, the brothers Charles and Ernest leased out all but the food departments, preferring to concentrate on what they knew best and letting other merchants take care of their business, all under Tiedtke's umbrella.

In July 1925, the Tiedtke brothers retired and sold the store to brothers Jerome and Alfred Kobacker, whose uncle operated Kobacker's furniture in Toledo. The Kobacker brothers had eyed Tiedtke's for some time, and they certainly appreciated the great institution that Charles and Ernest had created over the previous thirty-one years, for they left Tiedtke's name as they found it and changed few of the store's policies. Under their able management, Tiedtke's remained as popular as ever and cemented its status as a cherished Downtown Toledo destination.

In 1955, across the street at the corner of Summit and Adams, Tiedke's opened an annex dedicated to furniture in a building with a fascinating, if checkered, history. The J.L. Hudson Company, which was one of the nation's three largest department stores, became the dominant retailer of Detroit and the region surrounding it. Yet the store operated in Toledo in 1881, before it ever had an outlet in the Motor City. At the time, it was primarily a men's and boys' clothier but was a popular shopping destination in Toledo until a devastating fire in 1909 destroyed the building from which it operated. By this time, when Joseph L. Hudson had concentrated his efforts in Detroit, he was ready to exit the Toledo market. Before the embers on the site had cooled, however, a representative for the owner of the building vowed that "inside of 90 days you will see on this property one of the finest commercial buildings in the city."

An aspiring retailer named James Thompson in that year acquired an interest in Hudson's former business in Toledo, and in December 1909, when a handsome, new six-story building rose on the lot, ads proclaimed that Toledo had acquired a new dry goods store called the Thompson-Hudson

*The Store that buys and sells strictly
for cash and has no rent to pay.*

Tiedtke's store was deceiving. It's entrance was located on Summit Street, but most of the store was located on Water Street. *From an ad, collection of the author.*

Company. Later, Joseph Hudson sold his share of the store to two Cleveland businessmen, and it ultimately became known as the Rainie Barbour Company. Rainie-Barbour's came under control of the same Kobackers who owned Tiedtke's in 1928. The Kobackers changed the store's format to emphasize bargains and lower-priced merchandise and rechristened it as the "Fair Store" in 1932. The Fair lasted until the early 1950s, when Tiedtke's sought to expand its furniture department and took over the building for that purpose. Other businesses in this block included Sherman's Clothes, another Lane's drugstore, a pawnshop and Ruben's Oyster House.

Turning up Adams Street, the profusion of fashion stores lent a chic air to the shopping area, which extended west all the way to the Lasalle & Koch store at Huron Street. The ancient Trinity Episcopal Church, which looked as if it was hewn from rough stone, emphasized the street's status and added an air of dignity to the busy thoroughfare. Directly south of Trinity Church, on the other side of Adams Street, the Lion Store filled out the corner and served as a major attraction, anchoring the east end of the shopping corridor.

A view of the shopping district looking west on Adams Street. The tall Lasalle & Koch Company store rises on the left, directly across from the Paramount Theater's marquee. The McCrory's store on the left was Lasalle & Koch's second location before it moved to Jefferson and Superior Streets. *From a post card, collection of the author.*

Proceeding north, readers might remember that the sparsely detailed gold-brick building of the Willard Hotel housed street-level shops on the north side of Adams Street. Like all the businesses mentioned, the shops themselves changed as time went on, and any such revisit of Toledo's downtown core can only provide a snapshot of a given moment in time. For a long time, though, a Fanny Farmer candy shop was housed in the Willard, at the corner of Adams and St. Clair, and to its west were Dan-Chester Jewelers, Hanover Shoes, Flagg Brothers Shoes and Thom McAnn, with the hotel entrance right in the middle of them.

The national chain of men's shops, Richman Brothers, along with a Florsheim shoe shop, stood in a modernized four-story building across the alley just west of the Willard. Next door, local favorite B.R. Baker Company found its home on the corner of Huron Street in the 1927 Miniger Building with its formal, Adam-style stone detailing. Baker's, founded at 435–39 Summit Street in 1892 by Bernard R. Baker, changed its address to Adams Street in September 1931. From that point on, all that was the best in men's and boys' clothing could be had there. Jamie Farr said of B.R. Baker's: "Now that was a store I really liked! The class, taste and service found there were just first-rate."

In 1931, the B.R. Baker Company moved from Summit Street to the northeast corner of Adams and Superior Streets. *From a B.R. Baker advertisement, collection of the author.*

Though the founder died in 1942, the B.R. Baker Company was later led by his grandson, Bernard R. Baker II. Baker's friends often noted his conscientiousness and outgoing friendliness and that he always carried himself as a gentleman. A devout Catholic, he served in the navy during World War II and gave his time to a variety of charities; he worked tirelessly on behalf of St. Vincent's Hospital's funding needs. Under his leadership, B.R. Baker's tested new markets like Detroit and Cleveland and consistently maintained a top reputation among local retailers, despite the fact that Baker was also a full-time partner at his own law firm. His store reflected the qualities of its president and offered a high level of customer service to go along with the best in tailoring that Toledoans could count on.

In 1962, B.R. Baker's opened a "Baker's Casuals for Women" shop to appeal to the female customers who bought for their husbands at the store. Incidentally, Bernard Baker's wife, Elinor, to whom he had been married for sixty-one years at the time of his death in 2004, wrote society columns for the *Blade* under the pen name of Lynn Stevenson.

In 1961, the younger Baker stepped down to become chairman of the store when it was sold to Botany Industries of New York, a clothing concern that had bought up some of the country's finest men's stores, including Broadstreet's of New York, Harris & Frank of California and William H. Wanamaker, a men's clothier founded by the brother of the famous Philadelphia merchant John Wanamaker. Though it ceased to be owned by a Toledoan, B.R. Baker's reputation remained intact after the purchase.

The block across the street from Bakers, on the south side of Adams Street, held a variety of long-standing businesses sandwiched between downtown's largest S.S. Kresge store on the corner of St. Clair Street and an F.W. Woolworth branch at the opposite intersection to the west. The Kresge store was housed in a delightful, two-story building clad in terra cotta, and its lovely façades continued south around the corner down St. Clair Street. For many years, Park Lane hosiery and the Peggy Ann shop shared the building with Kresge's farther west on Adams Street while Burt's Shoes on the other side of the midblock alley was a part of the two-story edifice that also housed Woolworths.

Just across Superior Street from Woolworths, a buff-colored masonry commercial structure with a dark-colored cornice, ornamented by gargoyles, angels, floral wreaths and all manner of scrolls, was home to a large fashion store named Petries. Petries opened in September 1935 and called itself "Ohio's Most Beautiful Store." In fact, Petries was a part of a large clothing chain that at one time or another operated women's fashion stores under the names Marianne, Stuarts and Jean Nicole. Local retailer Davids for Fashion and the ubiquitous Morrow's Nut House, whose aromas of roasted nuts permeated the sidewalk outside, shared the building with Petries.

Lasalle & Koch's towering store, the western anchor of Adams Street, was just across the alley, but on the north side of Adams, the fabulous Paramount Theater, built in 1929, filled out most of the block, except for the large building at the corner of Superior Street that housed Bond's, a sizeable family clothing store that was a fixture in most downtowns through the 1960s. The building featured other street-level shops, such as Leo Marks Jewelers, Nisley's and Jack Lord.

The Paramount, which from time to time served as another event location for Lasalle's when its eighth-floor auditorium couldn't hold the anticipated crowds, was the grande dame of Toledo's theaters. The Paramount's cavernous lobby, clad in marble and draped in heavy fabrics, led to a balconied auditorium that sat over three thousand people; it was designed in the prevalent "Atmospheric Style," as a Spanish courtyard ringed by over-the-top Plateresque façades housing statuary and draped boxes. The ceiling simulated a nighttime sky complete with twinkling stars. Renowned theater designers Rapp and Rapp of Chicago were responsible for the design of the theater, which managed to be admirable and excessive at the same time.

On either side of its monumental marquee and vertical sign announcing, "Toledo Paramount," the building played host to other shops, most memorably Mark Klaus, the exclusive fashion salon that first opened in 1944. A United Shirt store held sway on the Huron Street corner where an earlier a Ligget's drug store and soda fountain served movie patrons.

The retail district transformed itself into an area of government buildings west of Lasalle's, though a few important retailers were located on the northern side of Huron Street at Adams. Next to Lasalle's on the west side of the street was a large Walgreen's drugstore, and on the other corner, the elegant and well-established Stein's ladies' apparel store rose like a punctuation mark signaling the end of the district, though a number of small shops and restaurants did thrive west of Huron Street. Stein's moved from Summit Street in the 1930s to its sophisticated, six-story home clad in limestone and detailed in the best Moderne fashion of the day.

The streets that crossed Adams held a wealth of smaller shops, restaurants and bank offices, too numerous to mention in this brief survey. Special notice should be given to a few of them, though, like the Broer-Freeman jewelry store on Jefferson and Erie Streets, in the same block as Lamson's. Broer-Freeman's elegant building was similar to Stein's in its suave and dignified style. Nearby, Smith's Cafeteria, with its selection of rooms on different levels, was a favorite place to take a meal in Downtown Toledo. Another interesting spot in downtown's heyday was the Richardson Building, at St. Clair and Jefferson Streets. Looking just like a handsomely conceived five-story office building, the 1925 structure was, in fact, a parking garage with retail space at the ground level.

As for the wealth of other businesses that filled out the streets, it is sufficient to say that the variety of bakeries, beauty salons, liquor stores, hardware shops, newsstands, hat shops and eateries of various types amounted to a rich banquet of choices that made Downtown Toledo the most complete shopping center of the day and more complete than any shopping mall, strip center or big box could ever hope to be, not to mention that the stores were more often than not locally owned and operated, helping to maintain the community's wealth. Moreover, our Three *L*s could never have been founded or have grown in isolation; they needed a home to become what they were at their apex, and Toledo was the ideal place for them.

Toledo Born—Toledo Owned—Toledo Operated

For much of its life, the Lamson Brothers Company promoted itself by reminding Toledoans that the store was "Toledo Born—Toledo Owned—Toledo Operated," a reference to the fact that Lasalle's and the Lion Store were owned by large New York interests. The slogan wasn't just hyperbole. Indeed, the Lamson brothers not only established their business in the Glass City but also kept it in their ownership throughout its duration, and the Lamson brothers themselves, while not native Toleodoans, had a heritage that dated back to the days of the Mayflower. Their family's history was characterized by slow but steady migration westward from New England until the brothers wound up in Toledo and established their store in 1885.

Descendants of one Barnabas Lamson, who left Harwich England in 1635, to settle in Newtone, Massachusetts (later Cambridge), the three Lamson brothers—Julius G., C. Edgar D. and John D.R.—were born in 1853, 1854 and 1859, respectively, in Elbridge, New York. Their father, Myron H. Lamson, had been born in 1823 in the small western New York town just north of the scenic Finger Lakes and later married the former Laura E. Rhoades. Myron was a wheelwright, and his Civil War service found him in Alexandria, Virginia, serving as assistant foreman of a team charged with constructing a new railway car for President Lincoln, which was hastily converted to a funeral car for the president directly after his assassination on April 14, 1865. The car was used to transport Lincoln's body to Springfield, Illinois, his final resting place.

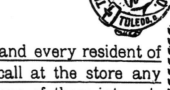
1908 Lamson Brothers ad offering Lincoln funeral car souvenir postcards to customers. The ad also contains the store's assurance that "if you see it in our ad, it's so." *Collection of the author.*

Years later, in 1908, to celebrate the forty-second encampment of the Grand Army of the Republic (GAR) in Toledo, Lamson Brothers issued a commemorative postcard bearing a photo of the black-draped railway car that had been preserved by Myron forty-three years earlier. The card itself, comparatively rare today, stated:

> *Now that a united nation reveres the memory of Lincoln and everything connected with his life and death, we thought it appropriate that we should present this picture to the brave men to whom our nation is so greatly indebted.*

Myron's sons Julius and Edgar left school shortly after the conclusion of Civil War hostilities to enter apprenticeship in retail businesses in Elbridge. In 1873, Edgar left to settle in Toledo, likely due to the presence there of other members of his mother's family. Upon Edgar's departure, his father allegedly (and prophetically) remarked, "One day I suppose people will see the name 'Lamson Brothers' over one of the biggest institutions in Toledo." He found work in the Bailey Brothers drugstore on the corner of Monroe and Summit Streets, and later at the Austin Y. Ladue Mill Supplies Company. His brother Julius left New York in October 1873 and found work at the Toledo dry goods business of Trepanier and Cooper. Interestingly, the Cooper name in this business was that of Frank H. Cooper, who left Toledo to found the Siegel Cooper Company of Chicago and, later, New York, one of the largest dry goods businesses of the day.

By 1880, Julius worked for Cohen & Koch, whose store was located at Madison and Summit Streets. The business lasted until Alfred Koch dissolved the partnership to go into business with Jacob Lasalle and ultimately form the Lasalle & Koch Company. Left without a partner, Cohen sold the business to S.H. Frank & Company, which moved the newly acquired stock to 333–35 Summit Street, and Julius Lamson continued his employment there. Edgar eventually joined him in the business, though before that, he had moved to Columbus in 1881 to work as a cashier for a railway company.

Julius, though, was ultimately unhappy with the changing fortunes of his employers and, in 1885, thought that he would be better off with his own business. Julius had married well. His wife, Katherine Tracey, was a member of a prominent Toledo family. It came to pass that her father, Doria, recognized Julius's ambition and reliability and offered to finance his son-in-law's venture.

Above: Souvenir postcard, issued by Lamson's, commemorating the Lincoln funeral car, built by the store founders' father. *Courtesy of Catherine Towle.*

Opposite: Portraits of the three Lamson brothers. *Courtesy of Catherine Towle.*

Julius G. Lamson   **C. Edgar B. Lamson**   **John D. R. Lamson**
of Lamson Bros., Dry Goods

Throughout Julius's experience in Toledo, his younger brother John remained in New York, working first in the same dry goods business as his brothers. Later, he moved to Syracuse and worked for a couple retail businesses, the final one of which was purchased by the Dey Brothers of Elmira, New York, and later became one of that city's premier department stores under their name. With Edgar in Columbus, Julius asked his brother John to come to Toledo to begin the Lamson business in earnest. Notably, both Julius and John were encouraged and aided with advice by both S.H. Frank in Toledo and the Dey brothers in Syracuse.

On October 6, 1885, the Lamson Brothers Company opened its doors at 319 Summit Street, in a twenty- by eighty-foot room without a basement or second floor. From these inauspicious beginnings, the Lamson Brothers' business embarked on a path of growth and expansion, a path often thought paved by the solid business principles and goodwill of the brothers who launched it. To illustrate, ads for the store in the early twentieth century carried both a daily weather report and the foundational slogan of the store: "If you see it in our ad, it is so." And another statement of policy, oft repeated, said, "From the first we have had but one aim, that is to give the people of Toledo the best qualities of merchandise at the lowest prices consistent with safe business policy." It can reasonably be assumed that the latter part of the claim referred to the nature of business at the time in a wildly growing Toledo. The names of various clothing and dry goods businesses came and went in the raucous atmosphere of a boomtown, but Lamson's was determined to stay and grow in the Glass City.

Within eighteen months, the premises was extended back to the Summit Street alley, with a basement and second floor, and by April 1889, the two

Lamson brothers' business bought out Julius's former employer, the S.H. Frank Company, and moved its operation to the former firm's location at 333–35 Summit Street. Doria Tracy's investment was fully repaid soon after the move, and Edgar returned to Toledo to join his brothers in business. The growth of the Lamson Brothers Company was such that additional frontage was acquired in 1897 and 1902, extending the store eighty feet up Summit Street toward Adams. The new buildings erected on these parcels for Lamson's reached a height of five stories. Eventually, in 1910, Lamson's Summit Street plant was extended by occupying the corner building at 345–47 Summit Street, which had housed competitor Lasalle & Koch's store before its move to the corner of Jefferson and Superior in 1899.

It was in this form that Lamson's grew up with Toledo, as a familiar and stable business, having been incorporated in 1905 and, in the eyes of its customers, living up to its motto of honesty and fair dealing. The store proudly advertised that it had customers with whom it carried on a mail-order relationship as far north as Alaska and as far south as the farthest tip of South America. The three Lamson brothers had done well for themselves. In 1915, however, the original partnership was broken by the death of John D.R. Lamson at the age of fifty-six. He was survived by his wife, Jenny, and four children.

With regard to the running of the Lamson Brothers Company, the void left by John's death was filled by Sydney D. Vinnedge, Julius's son-in-law, who joined the Lamson family by marring Miriam Tracy Lamson. The young Vinnedge took the post of director and vice-president and proved his worth to the company almost immediately. Yet even local newspapers concurred that Julius "was Lamson's more than his brothers." He outlived his brother John, and long after Edgar retired, Julius remained with the store he knew and loved.

A strict Baptist, Julius Lamson followed his religious convictions, not least in his administration of the store, which he saw as a paradigm of honesty and goodwill. To comply with the fourth commandment—"Thou shalt keep holy the Lord's day"—he ordered that the store's windows be draped from Saturday evening until the start of business on Monday morning. The store did not advertise on Sundays under his leadership, and these policies stayed in place after he retired in 1930 and even until after he passed away in 1942, just short of his eighty-ninth birthday.

Julius Lamson may have passed from the Toledo scene after watching his small, self-led business achieve legendary status in his adopted hometown. Fortunately, his family took up his place to keep Lamson's the store that was "Toledo Born—Toledo Owned—Toledo Operated."

The Lamson Brothers store on Summit Street. The smaller portion on the left is the oldest; the taller buildings are extensions to the store, which also took the corner building, once home to Lasalle & Koch's. *Collection of the author.*

The New Lamson Store

On a crisp spring day in April 1928, a little boy named Jules ran up to his grandfather and asked if he could put his foot on the shovel with which the older gentleman was prepared to break ground. The little boy was Jules Vinnedge, son of Sydney D. Vinnedge and his wife, Miriam, and the grandfather was none other than Julius Lamson himself, whose department store was ready to move from its Summit Street store to a new location and, in effect, begin a new era for the Lamson Brothers Company. Little Jules, whose association with his family's department store would have tragic consequences later in his life, was duly photographed for the event, which was preceded by months of preparation and deliberation by Lamson's management.

Toledo's retail business had been concentrated on Summit Street, but when Lasalle & Koch made the move two blocks north in 1900, it signaled not only the expansion of the downtown shopping district but also its removal from the venerable thoroughfare that housed long-established businesses such as Milner's, Thompson-Hudson, Tiedtke's, the Lion Store and Lamson's itself. The 1917 move of Lasalle & Koch's even farther north to Adams and Huron Streets essentially relocated the retail "spine" perpendicular to Summit Street and relegated the older shopping district to secondary status. By the late 1920s, Lamson's recognized this trend, along with the fact that its store—composed of a series of different storefronts and buildings—had become inadequate for the needs of an establishment that placed itself at the forefront of Toledo's retail offerings.

A youthful Jules Vinnedge helps his grandfather break ground for "Lamson's New Store" in April 1928. *By permission of the Toledo-Lucas County Library.*

After much study, a site on the northwest corner of Huron Street and Jefferson Avenue was identified as ideal for Lamson's expansion possibilities. While the site was somewhat remote from Adams Street, by then Toledo's main shopping street, it was only a short distance from Lasalle's large store and very near to the Commodore Perry and Secor Hotels, addresses that added cachet to the neighborhood and complemented the proposed facility very well indeed. For two years, the site was assembled quietly, and the building of "Lamson's New Store," as it was to be known, was announced on November 25, 1927. The 1927 announcement stated that the store would be among the largest in Toledo and would have frontage on Huron, Jefferson and Erie Streets. The architect of the Italian Renaissance–influenced edifice was identified as Mills, Rhines, Bellman & Nordhoff of Toledo, and it was noted that they were working along with Henry J. Spieker & Company, general contractors, to ready the building for occupancy in a year. The announcement also noted that the investment in the new building and its equipment alone would come close to $3 million.

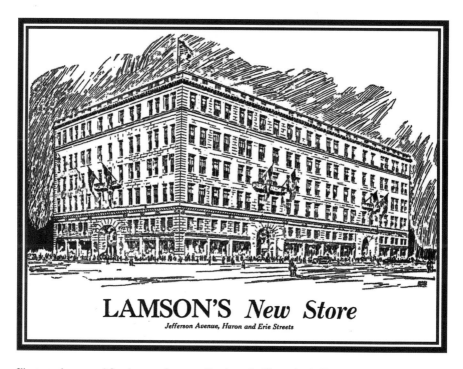

LAMSON'S *New Store*
Jefferson Avenue, Huron and Erie Streets

Illustrated proposal for the new Lamson Brothers facility to be built on the corner of Jefferson and Huron Streets in Toledo. *Collection of the author.*

After a delay of four months, the groundbreaking ceremonies were scheduled, and Toledo was able to watch the big new store take shape over the course of the next few months. The actual construction of the store must have been handled in record time, for it was readied for use by the next November, an almost unbelievable timetable for such an elaborate structure. The *Blade* noted with pride that the coordination skills of the Spieker organization were such that the work was often ahead of schedule by as much as fifteen to twenty days. Also noted was that "the contracts for [Lamson's] erection totaled approximately $2,750,000 and more than 50 per cent [*sic*] of these sub-contracts were awarded to Toledo firms. More than 70 per cent [*sic*] of all materials in the construction of the building were Toledo products or supplied by Toledo concerns."

By mid-November, Lamson's was able to advertise removal sales at the old Summit Street address and that the lower levels of its former store would be leased to the S.S. Kresge Company and McCrory's, everyday retailers more appropriate to Summit Street's somewhat downgraded status.

The process of moving personnel, equipment and remaining stocks was organized in great detail, so much so that after Friday's closing on Summit Street, the work could take place around the clock until the new Lamson's was ready for opening ceremonies on Monday morning, November 13. Newspaper reports stated that the Lamson's staff was organized "like an army" for the move and that it was made easier by the success of the enormous "removal sale" held in the weeks prior to the grand opening, which reduced the amount of material that had to be relocated.

On opening day, a "simple and dignified ceremony" was scheduled to follow an unveiling of the new store's twenty-one-window display. In his remarks, Julius promised, according to the day's reports, to "continue his policies of honesty and dependability, in strict conformity with the Golden Rule, which have been his policy since the founding of the business 43 years ago, and just as fully as they were when the store was founded at 319 Summit Street."

Lamson was then congratulated publicly by Mayor Jackson, who praised the store's role in the "upbuilding of Toledo" and the retailer's active participation in many civic enterprises and organizations. When the ceremonies proper were complete, the doors to the beautiful new building swung open, and the public was invited to inspect the merchandise and displays on offer until 9:00 p.m., serenaded by Seymour's orchestra, which played on the balcony overlooking the crowds pouring into the lofty street floor of the palatial new structure.

The store they perused was a five-story edifice with a full basement and extended 200 feet along Huron Street and 128 feet westward along Jefferson Avenue, embellished by three grandiose arched entrances. A two-story building adjacent to the new store was acquired and integrated into the facility, giving access to Erie Street as well. The Italian Renaissance design was accomplished with a very simple boxlike massing, enriched by the arched entrances. Its exterior was further characterized by elaborate detailing and luxurious materials.

The street façades of the New Lamson Store featured finely worked bronze-plated cast-iron framework around the display windows with the neutral piers between them faced in polished Minnesota Cold Spring rainbow granite likewise encased by frames of bronze. The rest of the building was clad in Indiana Oolithic limestone in a buff grade below the second-floor cornice and with variegated limestone sheathing the floors above. The beautifully detailed cornices, balconies and arched entrances of the store relieved the massing of the rectangular block, and the overall impression of the building is one of permanence and dignity with a touch of opulence liberally applied to hint at the retail luxuries inside.

The store's three main entrances, housed in deeply recessed Roman archways, deserve special mention. Two of these portals punctuated the Huron Street façade, but the one on the Jefferson Avenue side was slightly more elaborate, appropriate to Lamson's official address at 600 Jefferson Avenue. Flanking each arch were circular bosses depicting the symbols of six ancient merchant guilds of Florence, the art capital of Tuscany, which lies on the Arno River in the middle of the Italian peninsula. These symbols were chosen to enhance the decorative concept of the building, enhance its Italian Renaissance style and connect the Lamson enterprise symbolically with these old guilds, which stood for quality, craftsmanship and service. Newspapers, when describing the decorative stonework in the new edifice, commented as well that Florence and its symbols were appropriate for Toledo, which, with its glass-blowing industry and new art museum, sought to become an art capital in its own right.

The dignified New Lamson Store as it appeared not long after grand opening celebrations welcomed the Toledo public. *By permission of the Toledo-Lucas County Library.*

Now! ~ LAMSON'S New Store

Toledo's Modern New Retail Institution at Jefferson Avenue, Huron and Erie Streets

Program

Unveiling of Windows
11:30 in the Morning

President Julius G. Lamson
pledges continuation
of Lamson policies to Toledo
and Northwestern Ohio
in front of the
Jefferson Avenue entrance
11:45 o'clock

Toledo's Honorable Mayor
William T. Jackson
responds

Doors open 12 until 9
in the evening

Nothing will be sold
until Wednesday

Music by Seymour's Orchestra

FORMAL OPENING

Tomorrow ~ Tuesday noon *until* nine

THERE will be an opening at the NEW Lamson's tomorrow! This event has been looked forward to for years. It is the formal opening of the NEW store . . . and we are happy! A dream has come true, but if it were not for Toledo's faith in Lamson's, all of this human handicraft that has been wrought—all of the modern science and physical energy that have been combined could not have produced the great structure of steel and stone that stands at JEFFERSON AVENUE, HURON and ERIE STREETS.

There will be no transactions tomorrow. At 12 o'clock . . . the doors will be swung open to reveal to Toledo —and Northwestern Ohio, the beauty of this new store . . . its wondrous array of merchandise gathered from every corner of the world . . . its inviting atmosphere . . . its many new and welcomed service facilities! The executives, and employes unite in extending to you a sincere and cordial invitation to visit, and thoroughly inspect, Northwestern Ohio's most modern retail institution!

LAMSON'S

Grand-opening ad inviting customers to the ceremonies that would turn the new store over to the Toledo shopping public. *Collection of the author.*

Circular bosses representing guilds of Florence, Italy, on the 1928 Lamson Brothers store. *Photographs by the author.*

The guilds depicted on either side of the main Jefferson Avenue entrance include the "Dressers and Dyers of Foreign Cloth" and the "Mercers and Linen-Drapers." The first of these, to the left of the archway, depicts a fighting eagle clutching bales of cloth in its claws, symbolic of Lamson's status as a fashion store. The other, to the right of the archway, shows a fleur-de-lis and a large bale of cloth and would be understood in the sixteenth century as a mark of the retail trade.

On the southernmost of the Huron Street portals are depicted the symbols of the "Guild of Woolen Cloth Manufacturers," symbolized by a lamb with a pennant, and the "Guild of Silk Manufacturers," proudly bearing the Italian word "Seta" and symbolized by a locked pair of doors, which protect the guild's precious output. The former guild developed into a Roman Catholic religious order and can be seen as representing the Lamson family's deep and long-held Christian views while the latter was incorporated to reflect the quality and integrity of Lamson's business.

The twin entrance to the north is flanked by symbols of the "Guild of Furriers" and the "Guild of Butchers and Tanners," chosen to reflect the luxury products Lamson's offered and the shoe and leatherwear business, respectively. The symbol of the furriers is a shield with twenty-two facets, representing the twenty-two types of fur imported to Florence at the time, while the butchers and tanners are represented by a wild goat.

While the Erie Street Annex utilized an existing façade less elaborate than that of the main store, it housed the store's loading docks, ground floor storage and additional retail space. A second floor allowed Lamson's to provide medical facilities for employees in the new store.

Inside, the decorative refinement was no less present. Glass-and-wood display cases lined the walls and delineated the aisles of the lofty space, which provided a "straight-shot" promenade from the Jefferson Avenue entrance past beautifully displayed merchandise directly to six passenger elevators along the rear wall opposite. Each doorway was trimmed in darkly stained varnished wood, matching the display cases, and above each was an elaborately mullioned rose window of stained glass framed in decorative plasterwork. Octagonal columns culminated in decorative capitals with rope trim and floral patterns cast in plaster, and the ceiling was enriched with a bas-relief grid of rosettes surrounded by geometric patterns, softening the stark white ceiling by incorporating a gridlike pattern of decorative motifs running from column to column.

All these elements gave the new Lamson's an aura of spaciousness, height and elegance, cleverly calculated to facilitate the presentation and ultimate selection of high-quality goods. Merchandise offered on the first floor included accessories for women, jewelry, candy and men's furnishings. A passageway led to the annex where linens and fabrics were sold, and a balcony for musical performances overlooked the whole installation.

Upstairs, the New Lamson Store offered apparel for women and children on two intermediate floors and home furnishings on the fourth floor. Newspapers of the day waxed lyrical about not only the store's beauty but also its technical sophistication. Two freight elevators brought goods up from the loading docks to a fifth-floor receiving and marking room while a spiral chute was used to distribute merchandise back to the lower floors. An express chute for direct transmittal of outgoing orders to a delivery room far below was installed as well. *Toledo's Business*, in describing the New Lamson Store, stated that "extreme cleanliness throughout the building is of course necessary" and described the installation of a state-of-the art filtration and ventilation system with thermostats that guaranteed a constant temperature of seventy degrees as well as going into detail about the portable, truck-mounted vacuum-cleaner system.

Clearly, though it opened well after competitor Lasalle & Koch's and expanded its own monumental store in Downtown Toledo, the New Lamson Store proudly introduced innovations and technical installations, which, though they are hardly given a thought today, were models of their kind

The H.J. Nelson Company supplied interior furnishings for the store and illustrated its work in an ad congratulating Lamson's for its "modernity." *Collection of the author.*

in the pre-Depression era, and as a result, the reception of the store by the public was enthusiastic and generous.

Julius Lamson admitted that, since the death of his brother John and Edgar's retirement, he was "all alone." He noted also: "I came first, and I am here last. I am seventy-five. I will see it through. I will work out my years." In spite of his melancholy reflection on the occasion of his store's greatest achievement to date, he added, "We want our customers to know that we deeply appreciate their patronage. In the development of Lamson's, too, I feel that those faithful employees who have worked in various capacities for many years are deserving of commendation, and I extend it to them with the company's grateful appreciation of their loyal services."

On such a positive note, Lamson's was able to move forward to become perhaps Toledo's most fashion-focused and upscale department store. The looming depression, which was clearly accompanied by a struggle to survive, and a diminishing of optimism for the store and Toledo itself was ultimately overcome but not without sacrifice and great difficulty. Later years would see Lamson's settle comfortably into its role and become an integral part of Toledo's vernacular.

Toledo's Own Store

In 1929, after a career leading the store he founded, Julius Lamson was honored by the unveiling of a portrait of himself in the great store on Huron Street. The portrait was funded by donations from every one of Lamson's employees, and it was unveiled by none other than Jules Lamson Vinnedge, who helped his grandfather break ground for the vast structure over a year earlier. The portrait, which hung for many years opposite the Huron Street entrances to the store, was the work of artist Frank LaChance. To add to the honor, store vice-president W.E. Buckingham spoke, extolling Julius Lamson's fine personal qualities and informing him that the employees themselves, out of great respect for Lamson, conceived of the idea. Lamson, in his remarks, spoke of the great success that the store had experienced in its new home.

Almost a year later, Julius Lamson officially retired as president of the Lamson Brothers Company. True to his word, though, he remained as chairman of the board and retained an office in the store he built and so clearly loved. His son-in-law, Sydney Vinnedge, was promoted to president of the company. At the time of this transition, newspapers again celebrated the elder Lamson's contributions to Toledo life and, noting Vinnedge's presidency of the Toledo Chamber of Commerce and Toledo Retail Merchants board among other public service contributions, expressed the sentiment that Lamson's under such leadership would continue to grow and prosper in the Glass City.

The Lamson Brothers Company celebrated a golden jubilee on October 6, 1935, which was marked by the "Greatest Sale in the Store's History."

Newspapers recounted the store's history and growth and quoted semiretired Julius Lamson as saying that "50 years of contact with the Toledo public now brings us 50 years of happy memories." Lamson also went on to attribute the store's achievements to its adherence to "business principles which we have considered fundamental" and laud the "faithful cooperation of our personnel." The same article that described the anniversary also noted Julius Lamson's involvement in the Toledo YMCA and the Toledo Council of Churches, as well as his family's long membership at the Ashland Avenue Baptist Church.

By the time of the golden jubilee, Lamson's had taken advantage of increased space in the Huron Street building by adding a tearoom, a large men's clothing shop, bakery, optical shop, dry cleaning service and an extensive paint and wallpaper department. Toledo's growth, along with its acceptance of Lamson's, was truly worth celebrating.

Wendy Towle is a talented graphic artist based in the same geographic area where her Lamson ancestors settled. She keeps several trunks of Lamson memorabilia in her possession, and her mother, Catherine Towle, has preserved a history of the Lamson family, compiled by Wendy's great-grandmother Helen Lamson Ramseyer. Catherine is a living part of the Lamson's legacy and is proud to say she was a member of the Lamson family. Her great-grandmother was Jenny Lamson, John Lamson's wife.

Catherine Towle emphatically stated, "I was raised with the values of an upper-class family, although we were no longer really upper class. My grandmother Helen had sold her stock [in Lamson's] to help out my grandfather during the Depression. My upbringing really didn't have that much to do with the store."

Despite being from a somewhat distant branch of the family, throughout her life, she was proud to be a Lamson because the store was so well respected in the Toledo community. Catherine noted: "To this day I still brag a little that the Lamsons were my family, but that's all there is to it. They are my ancestors; the family was my grandmother's and my mother's but, in time, not mine, so I didn't know and had never met any of them. To me, the store was Grandma Helen's store. Nonetheless, the Lamson's [store] was very, very special to us."

Given that Lamson's effectively disappeared from the Toledo scene almost forty years ago, Catherine Towle's heritage and, indeed, her memories help to reinforce the value that this institution brought to Toledo at the time.

John McCleary, Catherine's cousin, was a well-known producer for WSPD, an NBC (later ABC) affiliate in Toledo. Though he left Toledo in 1972 to

LAMSON'S TEA ROOM

MENU
Service per person only
RELISHES

Mixed Pickles - - - 10	Hearts of Celery - - - 15	Sliced Tomatoes - - -	20
Queen Olives - - - - 10	Stuffed with Roquefort Cheese 30	Fruit Cocktail - - -	20

SOUPS (Ready to Serve)

Puree of Green Split Peas - - - 10   Clear Consomme, Cultivateur - - - - 10

CHEF: PIERRE BERARD RECOMMENDS THE FOLLOWING DISHES:

Poached Fresh Halibut, Oyster Sauce, Boiled Potato - - - - - -	45
Poached Eggs on New Spinach, Border of Potatoes, Mornay Sauce - - -	50
Hot Pork Sandwich, Mashed Potatoes, Vegetable Gravy - - - -	40
Vegetable Dinner Plate, Hollandaise Sauce 65; with Poached Egg - - -	75
Braised Lamb, Family Style, Potato Croquette - - - - - -	60
Roast Prime Rib of Beef au Jus, Boiled Potato - - - - - -	75

Bread and Butter Included with Above Prices

SALADS	DESSERTS	SANDWICHES	
Combination - - - 35	Apple Pie - - - - 10	Lettuce and Tomato	Ham and Cheese - 20
Hawaiian - - - - 35	Mince Pie, Hot or Cold 15	Sandwich - - - 15	Sardine - - - - 20
Waldorf - - - - - 30	Pumpkin Pie - - - 10	Ham - - - - - 15	Bacon and Tomato - 20
Chicken - - - - - 50	Cherry Pie - - - - 10	Swiss Cheese - - - 15	Bacon and Lettuce - 20
Fresh Shrimp - - - 50	Cocoanut Layer Cake 10	American Cheese - 15	Tunafish Salad Sand-
Lettuce and Asparagus 30	Cheese Cake - - - 15	Salmon Salad Sand-	wich - - - - 20
Lettuce and Tomato 25	Fruit Jello with Cream 10	wich - - - - - 15	Cream Cheese, Nut
Lettuce and Egg - - 20	Baked Apple 15, cream 20	Peanut Butter Sand-	and Jelly - - - 20
Salads Served with	Rice Pudding - - - 15	wich - - - - - 15	Cold Beef Sandwich 25
Mayonnaise, Russian or	Cup Custard, Vanilla	Ham Salad Sandwich 15	Cold Pork Sandwich 25
Thousand Island Dress-	or Chocolate - - 20	Fried Egg Sandwich 15	Corned Beef Sandwich 25
ing, 10c extra	Assorted French Pas-	Sliced Egg Sandwich 15	Fried Ham or Bacon 20
Head Lettuce - - - 25	try - - - - - 15	Egg Salad Sandwich 15	with Egg - - - 25
Sliced Tomatoes - 30	Danish Pastry - - 10	Sliced Tomato Sand-	Hot Pork Sandwich - 30
Cole Slaw - - - - 25	Fruit or Pound Cake 15	wich - - - - - 20	Chicken Salad - - 35
Vegetable Salad - - 40	Orange Ice - - - - 10	Cream Cheese and	Hot Roast Beef Sand-
Sliced Tomatoes - 30	Vanilla Ice Cream - 15	Chopped Olive - 20	wich - - - - - 35
Celery, Onion Salad 50	Chocolate Ice Cream - 15	Chopped Ham and Egg 20	Chicken - - - - 45
Fruit Salad - - - 40	Strawberry Ice Cream 15	Tongue - - - - 20	Club Sandwich - - 50

All Sandwiches, made on White Bread or on Whole Wheat, Graham, Rye or Raisin, plain or toasted on request

---

LUNCHEON 75 CENTS	LUNCHEON $1.00	LUNCHEON 85 CENTS
Soup or Health Cocktail	Soup	Soup, Fruit or Health Cocktail
Broiled Fresh Mackerel, Lemon	Lime Fruit Cup or Health Cocktail	Halibut Steak, Fresh Shrimp Sauce
Butter, Home-made Corned Beef	Creamed Crabmeat on Toast	Roast Leg of Veal with Dressing
Hash, Tartar Sauce	Minute Steak, Pear Fritter	Smoked Beef Tongue cook-
Italian Pot Roast with Spaghetti	Field Grill Baked Chicken Pie	ed with Fresh Spinach
Scrambled Eggs with Bacon	Roast Prime Rib of Beef	Curry of Lamb with Rice and
German Style	Buttered Squash	Tomatoes
Vegetable Combination	Long Branch Potatoes	Scalloped Tomatoes
Mashed Yellow Turnips	Head Lettuce, Roquefort	Dried Sweet Corn
or	Opened-faced Apple Pie with Wal-	Raisin-Celery-and-Apple Salad
Green Beans	nuts, Chocolate Pudding, Whip-	Prune Pie, Whipped Cream
Pumpkin Pie Ice Cream	ped Cream, Butterscotch	Chocolate Pudding, Whipped Cream
Preserved Figs, Molasses Cookies	Almond Sundae	Ice Cream
Coffee Tea Milk	Coffee Tea Milk	Coffee Tea Milk

BREADS

Whole Wheat, Toasted - - - 10	French Toast - - - - - - 25	Dry or Buttered Toast - - - 10
Cinnamon Toast - - - - 10		Toasted English Muffins - - - 15

BEVERAGES

Coffee - - - - - - - - 05	Cocoa or Chocolate - - - 15	Iced Tea or Coffee - - - - - 15
Tea with Cream or Lemon - - 10	Iced Cocoa or Chocolate - - - 20	Buttermilk - - - - - - - 15
Rock River Farm Certified Milk, bottle - 10	Malted Milk - - - - 20	All Sodas - - - - 15

All portions to be served for one, or a service charge of 10c is to be made otherwise

To give you the quickest possible service only items listed on this menu are served in this room

NOTICE: We regret that we cannot be responsible for hats, coats or other effects

Monday, November 24, 1930   H. C. Gordon, Managing Director

SEE REVERSE SIDE FOR FOUNTAIN MENU

Lamson's Tea Room menu from 1930. From the Business & Industry of Greater Toledo Collection, Toledo-Lucas County Public Library.

settle in Tucson, Arizona, where he taught at the University of Arizona, he remembers the trappings of growing up in a family that, in Toledo, was known as a "department store dynasty":

When I was a boy, we'd go downtown in my grandmother's Cadillac Sixty Special limousine, which would pull up to the canopied entrance on Jefferson Avenue, where a uniformed doorman would open the door and escort us into the store. Once inside, I couldn't help but be impressed by the elegant plasterwork on the ceilings, and if the shopping trip included lunch in the tearoom, that was very elegant, too. Even riding in the ornate elevators was special. We never shopped anywhere else. I visited it again when I came back to Toledo for my fiftieth high school reunion, and it was just as I remembered it—it was truly quite a place.

John McCleary went on to tell how Helen Lamson Ramseyer, his grandmother, saved their branch of the family by selling her Lamson's stock to purchase rental properties around the city, providing a stable source of income during the Depression. He also recalled hearing his grandmother telling stories of the days when their family had a private railway car that would take them on vacation to Arizona (not even a state at that time), which was an ideal place for her to rest and get exercise, since she suffered from rheumatic fever. One of the hilarious stories she told was of an excursion she took into the desert when the horse she was riding ran amok and brushed up against a large cactus that pulled off part of her hair. "Grandmother claimed she was the first woman in America to be attacked by a cactus!" John recalled.

Though their family became separated from the department store business due to his grandmother's divestiture of her stock, Helen Ramseyer often spoke of having tea at the Colonial Revival home of Julius Lamson on Scottwood Avenue in Toledo's West End and went to the house after his death when he lay in state. "It was interesting to grow up around those people, even though, after some time, our family wasn't living the lifestyle," said John. He also noted that his grandfather Maynard Ramseyer was a well-known builder in Toledo, as were members of his father's family. When his parents married, they brought two famous Toledo building families together. Like the Lamsons, they were all Baptists and their strong faith got them through the privations of the Depression.

Sarah Hogoboom, though she lived in Madison, Wisconsin, for most of her life, was born in Toledo eighty-five years ago. She spent summers with

Ohio relatives and speaks fondly of her memories of not just shopping trips but also items she received in the mail from the Three *L*s: "Over the years, many packages arrived at our Madison home from these Toledo stores. I remember especially the lovely things Aunt Jean sent for my trousseau from Lamson's: a pink silk nightgown and peignoir, a pretty white nightgown and white satin Daniel Green slippers to wear for the wedding, all packed between layers and layers of tissue paper."

The growth of Toledo and the resulting sprawl of the city, fueled by the development and growing popularity of the automobile, made retailers recognize, sooner or later, that people would be living farther and farther from their downtown flagship stores. In June 1943, when Toledoans scoured the papers for news of World War II and ration-card schedules, those same newspapers featured articles that looked ahead to a postwar era, when the nation would be at peace and the country could invest in progress. Ahead of its time, Lamson's announced that it would open a store in nearby Maumee, Ohio, in the premises of a former local department store and the adjacent building, which previously housed a grocery store.

When the actual opening of the store on the northwest corner of Maumee's Conant and East Wayne Streets was announced for July 31, 1943, it was with the caveat that "owing to wartime conditions, Lamson's Maumee is not as completely remodeled as we would have liked." The store's ads reinforced that "you have but to shop Lamson's Maumee to know that the same sound business principles prevail which have made the name 'Lamson's' synonymous with integrity, courtesy, and dependability [so that] we think you'll find shopping here both pleasant and convenient." The building itself was a rambling brick structure with a corner turret, mansard roof and a lively façade punctuated by multiple gables with deep rakes overhanging wood-trimmed bay windows. The street floor featured display windows that offered a glimpse into the new store and the treasures it held.

The local press described the enthusiastic crowds that greeted the store on its opening, noting that it featured "beautiful displays of fine merchandise" and that the archway connecting the two buildings afforded a vista through the store from its main entrance on East Wayne Street. An article found the store to be "beautifully decorated" by baskets of floral arrangements sent as congratulations by local merchants and friends of Lamson's.

An interesting sidelight accompanied the opening of Lamson's first branch store. By this time, Lamson's bakery had become well known throughout Toledo, if not most of northwestern Ohio, as a purveyor of the finest in baked goods. The store wanted to sell its delicacies in Maumee but, due to

Rare old photo, from an advertisement, of Lamson's Maumee store. *Collection of the author.*

wartime restrictions, could not do so without petitioning the Rationing Board of the Office of Price Administration for an increase in rationing points for the new location. Local citizens petitioned the board on Lamson's behalf, stating that manpower shortages during the war had caused several local bakeries to shut down and that there was a "severe need in the community for an adequate dispensary of baked goods." Upon approval, Lamson's was only too happy to stock its bakery counter with fresh items shipped daily from its Downtown Toledo bakeries.

After the cessation of hostilities, Lamson's sought to serve its expanding home market as well, but economic recovery and adjustment after the war made it difficult to proceed, until the company proposed a new store in the Colony Shopping Center on Central Avenue, where it meets Monroe Street. On December 5, 1950, the store announced that it would remodel and occupy a twenty-thousand-square-foot building in the shopping district, which opened nine years earlier. The announcement indicated that the store would be a "complete department store with all types of merchandise."

Near the landmark Toledo Hospital, the Colony Shopping Center was a block of street-side shops with parking at the rear and originally housed a Walgreen's drugstore, an F.W. Woolworth five-and-dime, two food stores and numerous small shops in its neocolonial brick buildings trimmed with stone ornaments. An eponymous art deco jewel of a cinema, the Colony Theater, brought entertainment to the area, and a bar and several restaurants completed its offerings.

The Colony suffered a devastating and lethal fire in 1944, which took the life of firefighter James P. Fakehany, who was pinned in the basement of the structure after part of the Woolworth and Kroger store walls collapsed, trapping him in the inferno. The fire began when a spark ignited chemicals during routine cleaning of bowling pins in the building's basement. The namesake theater was not damaged in the blaze, and the shopping center was rebuilt afterward. Various other retailers were located on the adjacent streets, making the Colony an attractive and popular postwar shopping spot in Toledo.

Construction scheduling was apparently not as fluid as in 1928, when Lamson's was able to build its large flagship store in a remarkable seven months' time. Lamson's Colony opening had been projected for the spring of 1951, but it did not open until November 9 of that year. Even at this later date, newspapers and Lamson's ads warned that the new store (in fact Toledo's first branch department store) would not be complete until "early next year," and the store opened without offering ladies' fashions, appliances or any home furnishings merchandise.

Nonetheless, Lamson's "threw open the doors" to the new store on the crisp November day, and thirty thousand customers turned out to see it, complete or not. Those customers were given gifts of balloons (for children) and fresh roses (for women), while being entertained by the Glenn Trio. Toledo mayor Ollie Czelusta noted the store's two thousand parking spaces and prophesized that Toledo would need more auto-centered developments in the future. Back downtown, on the same day, the Commodore Perry Hotel's Shalimar Room advertised dinner and dancing to Jack Staulcup and "his celebrated orchestra," the Paramount Theater showed *A Streetcar Named Desire* and Lamson's ads for the day announced that the store was ready for the upcoming Christmas season, proclaiming, "The more the merrier Christmas at Lamson's."

In March of the next year, with the whole store completed, Lamson's held a "Gala Open House" with similar trappings to the earlier opening. Lamson's ad announcing the open house, which called the store "one of the loveliest, most modern suburban stores in Ohio," also listed the new departments and thanked the store's contractors for their work, as well as customers "who have been so patient with our building and expansion stages." In fact, the store referred to the new branch as "another milestone in Lamson's Parade of Progress."

Grand opening advertisement for Lamson's new Colony store. *Collection of the author.*

The term "Parade of Progress" also referred to the modernization, expansion and remodeling of Lamson's flagship store in the early fifties, where, floor by floor, the store was updated. New retail space was occupied on the fifth floor, and an adjacent building on Jefferson Avenue became the store's new enlarged men's store. Jamie Farr, whose mother worked as a milliner for a time at Lamson's, when asked to describe his experiences at the store, stated that, though he did occasionally shop there, "I thought of it as more of a ladies' store—the atmosphere seemed mostly feminine." Likely, Farr's impression was due to Lamson's relocation of men's merchandise outside the store's main building.

Another "float" in this parade was the Parkway Plaza store on Anthony Wayne Trail at the corner of Detroit Avenue in Maumee. Twice as large as the Colony store of three years earlier, the branch anchored a strip shopping center that was among the first auto-oriented plazas in the Toledo area; in fact, ads and articles didn't focus as much on the amenities of the center as much as the 1,200-car parking lot that it provided for customers.

Nevertheless, Lamson's put on a fine grand opening on March 11, 1955, substituting fresh orchids for the roses given to ladies at the previous event for the Colony store. The single-floor store with its dramatic and decidedly modern overhanging canopy, emblazoned with the Lamson name in large, halo-lit script on its face, made a huge impression on the public, and the *Toledo Times* took delight in describing the

> *dramatic use of color and interior decorating techniques. Grey fixtures have been placed against a background of soft, muted pastel shades which cleverly partition each department as well as give an illusion of space. Columns in each area pick up the coloring of the background wall….Numerous ingenious display ideas have been created to call attention to individual departments. Each is set off with a decorative motif on the pastel wall backdrop, high enough to be visible and readable from any part of the store. The only departure from this decorating scheme is the men's furnishings and men's sportswear departments. Both are decorated with a background of painted redwood.*

A photograph taken at the time of the new store's opening shows display counters just inside the entry filled with cakes and pastries, an indication of the prized role the store's bakery still played to Toledo customers.

Lamson's, with three (admittedly small) branch outlets in the Toledo area, was the only big department store to open stores in the growing outskirts

Interior (top) and exterior (bottom) views of Lamson's Parkway Plaza store. *Courtesy of Wendy Towle.*

of the city. Downtown was still a magnet for shoppers, and Lasalle's and the Lion Store felt confident enough in that fact to expand beyond Toledo into other northwest Ohio cities rather than open local branch stores. With three such stores in the city and its environs, Lamson's would wait more than fifteen years before planning another branch store to help expand its customer base in the Toledo area.

Toledo's Franklin Park Mall opened in July 1971, though few Toledoans know that its name is a clue to the sprawling shopping center's history. The Franklin in the moniker refers to Toledo's long-gone Franklin Creamery, an ice cream and candy manufacturer that retailed its treats at stores in Toledo, Cleveland and Monroe, Michigan. Founded in 1922, the company opened a new plant in 1940 on 110 acres at 5015 Monroe Street near Talmadge, northwest of Downtown Toledo. The company also developed the site as a secondary airport known as Franklin Field.

In the summer of 1952, Irving Reynolds, president of the Franklin Ice Cream Company (also known as the Franklin Creamery), announced his intention to develop the property as a large shopping center. Plans called for a 330,000-square-foot "strip" style shopping center surrounded by 6,000 parking spaces, making it the largest development of its type in Toledo. These plans never materialized, though the project was revived several times in the 1960s. Incidentally, concurrently with the shopping center proposal, the airport closed, and its operations were transferred to the smaller National Airport, north of Toledo; ironically, that site was developed as Toledo's North Towne Mall in the late 1970s.

In 1964, Franklin Ice Cream Company was purchased by United Dairies of Cincinnati, which closed the company's plants in Toledo and Cleveland while still retailing ice cream under the Franklin name. In reality, though, Toledo lost another indigenous brand, as Franklin products were, going forward, manufactured in the Cincinnati area and trucked northward to retail outlets.

With the Franklin Creamery plant shuttered, development of the mall could proceed, but it wasn't until another abortive plan was put forth by the J.C. Penney Company that the project actually began construction in 1969. This time, it was visionary mall developer James Rouse who owned and promoted the newly named Franklin Park Mall, anchored by Detroit's J.L. Hudson Co., the J.C. Penney Company and Lamson's. In announcing his plans, Rouse stated that "the prospect of two of the finest merchants in the world, J.C. Penney and J.L. Hudson, coming together with Lamson's, challenges us to create at Franklin Park a marketplace and shopping atmosphere second to none in America."

Lamson's new store was a large investment and major achievement for the eighty-six-year-old company, and it was duly promoted on its July 20, 1971 grand opening with the slogan "And you should see us now!" Ads presaging

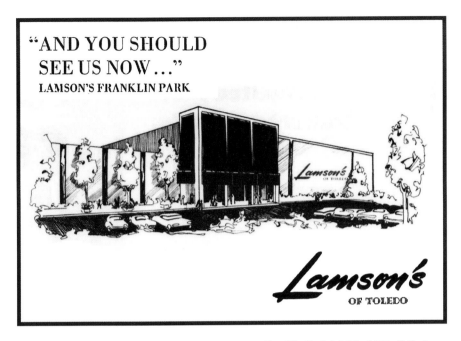

Advertisement illustrating the new Lamson's store at Franklin Park Mall in 1971. *Collection of the author.*

the company's ninety-thousand-square-foot store, its first full-line branch, touted the store's beautiful décor and deluxe merchandise.

With little archival material remaining, save the store's own grand opening advertising, it is difficult to get a true picture of Lamson's at Franklin Park. For that, though, it is possible to rely on a detailed memo written by Detroit-area retail and marketing consultant Frederick Marx, who visited the store while on a scouting trip for Michigan retailer Jacobson's, which was considering a Toledo branch at the time. Marx stated:

> *The Lamson building at Franklin Park Mall is most handsome and impressive, inside and outside. The traditional design has an enduring quality which will become adaptable to future decades and their trends. The location, focusing toward Talmadge and the Ottawa Hills environs, is ideal…it provides a separate entrance, away from the hubbub of activity which is currently a part of the mall's tenant-mix, and hosts surface parking in abundance. The interior format of the structure is attractive; the shoe salon is portrayed most attractively with Gloria Vanderbilt–type wallpaper and sofa fabric to match…and this comes off akin to the gracious setting one associates* [with Jacobson's].

With the Franklin Park Mall store, Lamson's didn't just look to reinforce its traditional image as Toledo's fashion leader with fine décor and an emphasis on high-style merchandise. It also looked toward the future, when full-service branch stores would be the norm.

Lamson's flagship downtown underwent another update at the time of Franklin Park's opening to keep up with current merchandising trends. Earlier, some of the less impulse-driven merchandise on the store's main floor had been moved to the basement (in the case of housewares) or to the fifth floor (gift shop, china and table linens). The basement was remodeled in 1971 into a so-called Lower Level, which housed a smaller Budget Store along with the departments relocated to it a few years earlier. At the time, these changes were seen as giving Lamson's a thoroughly modern, up-to-date merchandising strategy that would bode well for the locally owned company.

A result of Lamson's desire to promote the downtown store as a viable and attractive shopping destination, in spite of declining retail sales experienced by the district in general as shopping center development accelerated, was "Huron 200," an event sponsored by stores along the stretch of Huron Street that connected Adams to Jefferson. Special events, hourly prize drawings and sales by various stores, including Lamson's, were an attempt to draw attention to the location as an upscale and unique shopping experience.

Yet the march to the suburbs could not be ignored. A little more than a year after the opening of Franklin Park Mall, Lamson's presented the public with an 82,000-square-foot branch store in Southwyck Mall on Reynolds Road in southwestern Toledo. Developed in part by the Lion Store's owner, Mercantile Stores, Inc., Southwyck was the retail portion of the multimillion-dollar Hawthorn Hills planned community that surrounded the mall's property. Southwyck, the brainchild of Leon Winbigler, president of the Lion Store, came to house a Lamson store because of the strength of marketing surveys undertaken by the company, which, at the time, already had a store under consideration at Franklin Park. Jules Vinnedge, Lamson's president, stated at the time of Southwyck's opening on August 2, 1972, that the "survey gave us the facts to open Franklin Park, and also to commit ourselves to Southwyck at the same time."

Lamson's new store was only a stone's throw from its Parkway Plaza branch but was twice the size and better able to serve the modern Lamson customer with a wider range of departments. Newspaper reports noted the unusual parallel arrangement of the up-and-down escalators in the store, as well as mentioning an exhaustive list of its departments, including a large

Lamson's Southwyck store, as depicted in an advertisement from August 1972. *Collection of the author.*

beauty salon and travel services, and its décor, similar to that of the Franklin Park store, "with unusual wallpaper and fabrics and chrome fixtures." An example of the way that department stores of the time sought to introduce the "store-within-a-store" concept was the young men's "mod shop," introduced at the Southwyck store named "Ego-Men-Triks!"

With its well-positioned branch stores and a still-relevant downtown flagship, Lamson's would appear set to compete in the new world of retail in the 1970s. The company invested in its physical plant and sought to maintain its role as Toledo's traditional fashion leader, a cut above its competitors and a favorite of well-heeled Toledo shoppers. Yet that new world included competition that the store didn't expect, a changing economy dominated by energy concerns and a Toledo that was itself in a state of transformation.

What's in a Name?

I n addition to being the oldest of the Three *L*s, the Lion Store was a most fascinating example of a department store that didn't go by its founder's name. Los Angeles's the Broadway was named after the street on which it was located, and New Orleans's Maison Blanche took a fairly common name for department stores, "White House." The Lion Store's nomenclature shifted from that of its founder, Frederick Eaton, when the installation of a pair of cast-iron lions on either side of its front door on Toledo's busy Summit Street caught the imagination of its customers.

On the occasion of the eighty-second anniversary of the store in 1939, the *Toledo Blade* reminisced that

> [the lions] *have seen cobblestones change to smooth pavement and have marked the passage of hoop-skirts and bustles through hobble-skirts to knee-high skirts back to bustles again. They have noticed that the little boys who climb astride their backs no longer wear long curls and sailor suits. They have missed the horses which used to wait restively at the curb for their owners to return to the buggies. And they have seen the skyline of the city change, the traffic thicken, and have unblinkingly noted the hum of airplanes where only birds flew in their earlier days.*

Before the lions arrived, however, the store had its own interesting history, but unlike the Lamson Brothers Company, the history of its founder is more difficult to trace given the lack of locally held records or vocal histories by

TOLEDO'S
best-known
LANDMARK

—the lions
that have
identified
Toledo's best-
known store

---ever since 1857!

1930s ad promoting the lions that had become Toledo landmarks. *Collection of the author.*

surviving members of a family. The store was founded in 1857, when one Frederick K. Eaton opened the doors of his dry goods business on Summit Street. Eaton, who was born in February 1836, arrived in Toledo, then only twenty years old, from Sutton, New Hampshire. In his hometown, he had worked in a dry goods business and achieved an income of $300 dollars per year after moving to nearby Manchester. History doesn't record his reasons for choosing Toledo as the next stop in his life's adventure, but his brother

John's presence there and the city's growth potential clearly were factors in his decision.

After two apparently unsatisfactory attempts at employment in the Glass City, then known colloquially as "Frogtown" due to its swampy location, Eaton decided to open his own business at 115 Summit Street, in partnership with his brother John Eaton Jr., who had been superintendent of the city's public schools. The opening of the store in September 1857 makes the Lion Store one of the oldest department stores in the country, ranking fifteenth behind such illustrious names as Lord & Taylor (1826), Jordan Marsh (1841), Macy's (1842), Gimbels (1842), Lazarus (1851) and Marshall Field & Company (1852).

At the time, Toledo was in the throes of a major recession. Nevertheless, the small one-room Frederick Eaton & Company found success despite the economic climate, no doubt partially due to the fact that it had been financed only by the savings of the partners, who reportedly slept in the store as a guarantee against fires and burglaries. Within a year, the store moved slightly south to larger premises at 79 North Summit Street. The reference to addresses can often be unclear due to the city's change of the street numbering system in 1888, but the store moved again in 1863 to the corner of Summit Street and Madison Avenue. Outgrowing this location, the business was moved back down the street to 169–71 Summit Street, a location that would later become the site of Toledo's large W.L. Milner & Company store.

In 1866, however, Eaton would move the store to its ultimate location on the street known as "Toledo's Grand Promenade," 325 Summit Street. At this time, the original Eaton store was known as the "Bee Hive" on account of the customer traffic in and out of the store. The new premises in the block between Adams and Madison primarily housed the store's wholesale departments.

It is around the time of the move to 325 Summit Street that the lions appeared, though their history is likewise somewhat unclear. One of the oldest references to the lions dates them to 1872, when the wholesale store burned to the ground and a new four-story building was put up in its place. This report also sources the two lions as being cast in the old James & Kirtland foundry in the Bronx, New York. The foundry achieved fame by casting the iron structural members for the dome of the U.S. Capitol in Washington, D.C.

This version of the lions' gestation states that Eaton, who had, at the time, moved the retail operation into the new building and relegated the old Bee Hive to wholesale operations, was looking for a way to attract traffic

Detailed view of one of the Lion Store's mascots. *By permission of the Toledo-Lucas County Library.*

to the new location. Visiting the circus with his family, Eaton noticed that the trained lions attracted the greatest crowds and that, while people were terrified of them, they couldn't help but be mesmerized by the powerful beasts. The experience was the inspiration for his cast-iron lions, which he placed in front of the store as a sentinel and a curiosity.

Because of existing references to the long-gone James & Kirtland foundry, the story sourcing the lions from New York is most likely correct, but another fact goes a long way toward confirming it. This account also states that an identical pair of lions was purchased by a wealthy woman to beautify the entrance to her estate on Fairy Island in Lake Mahopac, New York, north of the Bronx. Brian Vangor, Carmel town historian (in which Lake Mahopac is located), has verified that the lions are indeed there, albeit with a coat of brilliant white paint. From photographs, it can be determined that the pair is quite identical to its siblings that made their home in Toledo for so many years.

The other version of the story states that the lions came one at a time from Massachusetts and Chicago, respectively, which accounted for the one-hundred-pound difference in their weights and the variations in their appearances, one of which was described in the store's employee newsletter (known as "Lion Tales") as having "a decidedly pussy-cat expression." A

Late 1800s view looking south down the three hundred block of Summit Street. The Lion Store is in the center, and one of the lions is barely visible near the entrance to the building, which served the store for over 108 years. *By permission of the Toledo-Lucas County Library.*

gentleman by the name of Robert Leibius, who in 1938 was the oldest living employee of the Lion Store, stated to the *Blade* that he recalled the lions being there before he began employment at the store in 1872. The accounts that date the lions prior to the 1872 building at 325 Summit Street indicate that they moved from location to location with the store. However, the newer store is the only one with a record of being called "Lion Store," and by this time, Eaton had taken on a partner by the name of Asa Backus. Newspaper accounts at the time referred to it as the "Eaton & Backus Lion Store."

Whatever their provenance, it is undisputed that the stately, bronze-plated beasts drew attention to Eaton's business and that the store's popular name overtook its formal one as a result of their presence on pedestals outside the store's main Summit Street entrance. Equally true is that they were the stuff of legend in a growing Toledo. When Downtown Toledo, and particularly Summit Street, was the city's premier shopping district, hardly a child grew up without sitting on the sturdy backs of the Lion Store's mascots, and from the time they arrived, stories about them have filled the annals of Toledo history. A contemporary of the aforementioned Robert Leibius was working at a freight depot at the time and recalled that the circus was in town on the day before the cast-iron lions arrived in Toledo. A major commotion occurred when an unsuspecting worker was scared out of his wits to see a pair of lions staring at him after he rolled open the door of a freight car, making him think he had mistakenly opened the door to the circus train's lion car.

For years, fraternity and sorority pledges scrubbed the lions and polished their fangs as an initiation task. Drunks turned the corner and fled in the opposite direction when they saw them standing guard on their pedestals, and many are the stories of customers, who, busied with the task of shopping at this favorite among Toledo's department stores, noticed only too late that their small child had wandered off. More often than not, the child could be found outside the Summit Street door, happily in the company of these inanimate replicas that had taken on a life of their own.

The lions themselves have been a part of Toledo lore during the years that they held court on Summit Street. Their very presence was threatened in 1949, when Toledo passed an ordinance forbidding curb signs, but due to public outcry over the fact that the law would have forced the removal of the city's favorite mascots, the law was rescinded and rewritten to forbid only new curb signs and protect the bronze-covered beasts at their home on Summit Street. Another tale, reported in the *Toledo Blade* in 1948, recounted how the mayor of a nearby town, who was in his cups after spending some time at a downtown bar, jumped on one of the stationary lions with the ridiculous hope of outrunning a policeman who pursued him for questioning. So embarrassed was the politician, who went nameless in the press, that he had himself fined for drunken conduct on the next day back in his home jurisdiction.

One of the most notorious episodes in the lions' history occurred in 1955, when one of them was reported missing in May of that year. The next day, the members of the Sigma Alpha Epsilon fraternity on the University of Michigan Campus in Ann Arbor, about fifty-five miles away, woke up to find the fifteen-hundred-pound feline in their living room. When questioned about the disappearance, members of the same fraternity at Toledo University claimed no responsibility but did relate how the Lion Store had once presented the organization with a papier-mâché replica of one of its mascots as a commemorative gift and that the fraternity and its brother organization in Michigan had taken turns "raiding" each other's house and snatching the replica. After some consternation on the part of university authorities in Ann Arbor and Toledo, the lion was returned to its Summit Street perch. Interestingly, the *Toledo Blade* reported that in Ann Arbor "no one seemed to know how it got there. At least nobody wanted to say."

On another occasion, in 1970, one of the lions went missing after being hit by an unattended car left running on Summit Street in winter. It was absent from its granite pedestal for a month while being repaired.

One of the most poignant existing tales about the lions, however, from a twenty-first-century perspective, regards a story contest held by the Lion Store in 1945. In announcing the winner of the contest, the store's "Lion Tales" employee newsletter wrote:

> *If the lions could only talk…we've thought many times. Then an idea was born. The lions cannot talk…but the people who know them and love them can. Hence, our Lion Story Contest became a means by which to take an excursion into the memories of our friends and learn a little of the romance of the lions. And how the letters have poured in! We've read them all… we've laughed…we've cried. And we find ourselves with a great deal more awe and respect for our very experienced lions…and a renewed rush of pride for the store they symbolize.*

The first-prize winner was a Mrs. Charles Hotos of Perrysburg, Ohio, who told the story of a little blind girl who dearly loved the lions even though she was unable to see them. Surely the laughs mentioned in the quote above came from the tale told by a lady whose grandson asked her how old the lion on which he perched was. "Well, honey," she said, "they are a lot older than I am." "That may be," the little boy replied, "but I don't see any white hairs on him yet." Another parent reported that she found her (obviously precocious) son sitting backward, near the lion's derrière. When asked why he chose the position, the boy replied that "I sat this way because I didn't think he could bite me back here!"

It is not certain what caused the prize jurors to cry as reported, but one anonymous comment shared in the "Lion Tales" contest certainly could coax a tear today, when the Lion Store is but a memory and Summit Street a windswept open area devoid of the life it had for much of the nineteenth and twentieth centuries:

> *In this world of changes, it is a joy to know that some things remain constant. What a heartbreak it is to return to childhood scenes, held in memory for a lifetime, and find them all different than we expected. In "Toledo Tomorrow" I hope one scene of my childhood may remain intact. If for any reason the two lions in front of the Lion Store on Summit Street should be removed, it would leave a scar on the heart of every person who ever climbed upon them in childish glee.*

For the coming decades, though, the store continued to prosper, with the wholesale division, whose business was normally concentrated within a two-hundred-mile radius of Toledo, boasted of customers as far away as Texas. In 1885, George M. Fisher, a businessman who arrived in Toledo from St. Louis one year earlier, was taken on as partner, and the store name was changed to Fisher, Eaton & Company, though the "Lion Store" name persisted among the public. When Frederick Eaton died in 1890, Fisher bought both Eatons's shares of the store and renamed it the Lion Dry Goods Company.

Under Fisher's leadership, the Lion Dry Goods Company was acquired by the H.B. Claflin Company of New York, an early department store chain that was originally founded as a wholesale supplier to retail companies. Over the course of its history (it was begun in 1843 by Horace Brigham Claflin), the Claflin organization expanded by purchasing retail dry goods companies through several subsidiaries, including Associated Merchants and United Dry Goods; it was the latter of these that eventually owned Lion Dry Goods.

The acquisition of retail firms (which brought on a significant debt to the company) was a response to the trend of department stores to increasingly buy directly from manufacturers, weakening the market for Claflin's goods. Under the plan, the company could control its own customers and defeat the very trend that was limiting its sales. Ironically, its own department stores' competitors became less likely to purchase goods from Claflin due to its influence over their local rivals.

It was this involvement in the retail trade that led *Moody's* magazine to state, in retrospect, that Claflin "was building up a paper structure that a storm must inevitably bring down. The panic...started when someone asked for a real dollar instead of another promise to pay. The story is one of bad judgment in refusing to recognize economic changes and stretching credit to the breaking point."

The magazine, in analyzing the Claflin debacle, referred to its acquisition of stores like the Lion Dry Goods Company as "pyramiding."

In June 1914, Toledo papers reported on the fact that one of the city's biggest retail concerns fell into receivership, but the news was relegated to secondary status; the same week, heir to the throne of the Austrian Empire, Archduke Franz Ferdinand, and his wife, Archduchess Sophie, were assassinated in Sarajevo, Yugoslavia, igniting the conflagration that became known as the Great War. The Lion Store itself referred to its own situation in an ad published on June 29, 1914, informing its "Friends and Patrons":

> *To correct wrong impressions that may come about from a receiver having been appointed for our company—we wish it clearly understood: The store has not been closed on this account. The business will continue without interruption. Every courtesy extended our customers in the past, they can enjoy now, as though nothing had happened. Just continue to do your part, and we will do ours—and your "home store," over 50 years old, shall go on—shall we say forever.*

After months of legal actions, two viable firms emerged from the Claflin bankruptcy. The first, Associated Dry Goods, owned New York's Lord & Taylor as well as a number of retailers throughout the country, including Hengerer's of Buffalo, Stewart's of Lousiville, Powers of Minneapolis and Hahne & Company of Newark. The other retail chain was named Mercantile Stores Company, and it controlled a wide variety of well-known department stores such as McAlpin's of Cincinnati, Hennessy's of Montana, Castner-Knott of Nashville, Joslin's of Denver and the Jones Store Company of Kansas City. It is to this latter group that the newly renamed Lion Store belonged, and from this point forward, the store, while still thought of by the Toledo public as indigenous, was in effect controlled by the New York–based holding company of which it formed an important part.

There's No Place Like Home

In spite of the New York–based ownership by the H.B. Claflin Company, the Lion Dry Goods Company made every effort to portray itself as in touch with the Toledo customer it served. Ads referred to it as "the homelike store," or "Toledo's home store," and even until after the turn of the century, it occupied the four-story 1872 building that shared Summit Street with other established retailers such as the Thompson-Hudson Company, Milner's, Lamson's and Tiedtke's. The Lasalle & Koch Company moved off Summit Street in 1900, spreading the retail district northward.

In 1904, the Lion Store built a four-story addition to the west of its main Summit Street store. The new building, constructed in the Chicago style of commercial architecture and offering a sixty-foot frontage on St. Clair Street, was connected by tunnel and bridge across the alley to the older structure. While Summit Street, with its signature lions, remained the store's "front door," ads mentioned that the St. Clair Street entrance was ideal for waiting carriages and offered an alternative for those who "wished to avoid the traffic and crowds on Summit Street."

In April 1910, the store announced that it had acquired a lease to an existing three-story building on the corner of St. Clair and Adams Streets, known as the Trinity Building after the Episcopal church that stood across from it. This acquisition was adjacent to the St. Clair Street construction site on which the Lion Store was expanding its 1904 building and offered it an advantage no other Toledo department store had at the time: an entrance to its physical plant from three of the city's main streets.

Around the same time, the expanded St. Clair Street frontage was doubled with a matching addition to the north of the 1904 building. Though the expanded premises were completed in the spring of 1910, a formal opening wasn't announced until fall, in conjunction with the store's fifty-third anniversary. An unusual, full-page ad extolled the virtues of the new store, saying:

> *We have grown with Toledo in a way we and all Toledo are proud of—grown with the staff of honesty, integrity, and fair dealing firmly planted before us into a larger and more metropolitan store—ever guarding the confidence of its patrons as its most treasured possession. Only twenty-four hours have passed since the Formal Opening of Our Enlarged Establishment, and yet in this short interval it already stands for a new era in department store usefulness. Designed as it was for the convenience and comfort of our patrons—built for their service and stocked with splendid merchandise for their selection. We want you to know the Lion Store of today—we want you to feel that it is your store—a store you may place your confidence in—a store you are always welcome in—a store in which you may always feel at home. Your grandmother's store—your mother's store—your store—the newer and better Lion Store.*

On the next day, the store announced a formal "fashion opening," highlighting the store's new stocks of the cream of Parisian and American apparel, and noted proudly that the Lion Store's new fashion departments occupied the whole of its new St. Clair Street Building. By this time, the store's physical plant covered almost 120,000 square feet of space on four floors and a basement.

In September 1912, another construction project expanded the St. Clair building northward to Adams Street around the Trinity Building to provide another entrance and more frontage on Adams Street, and the Lion Store took the form it would have until the late 1920s. The various pieces built expressly for the store, because of their similarity, indicate that there may have been an early plan to fill out the whole block with a uniform modern store, four stories in height.

The Lasalle & Koch Company, after expanding its 1900 premises northward several times, boldly constructed a large new store at Adams and Huron. This move not only looked past the war raging in Europe to focus on the future but also led the future growth of Toledo's retail core and moved it decidedly westward. In 1928, after Lasalle's expanded its store at the new location,

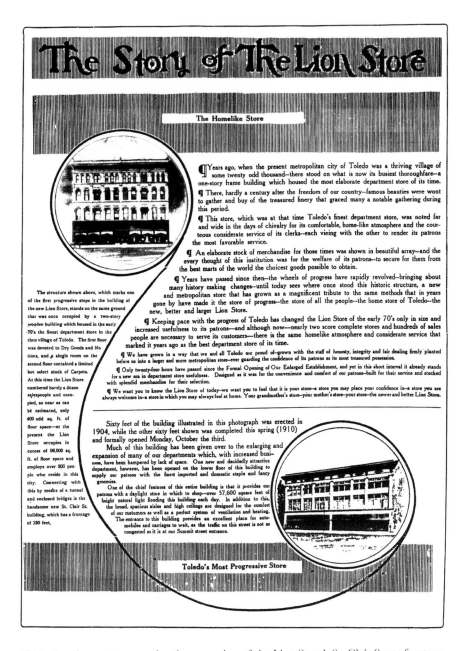

1910 advertisement announcing the expansion of the Lion Store's St. Clair Street frontage to 120 feet. *Collection of the author.*

Illustration used in Lion Store ads from the 1920s. While not strictly accurate, it did give customers a clue to the layout of the various buildings occupied by the store. *Collection of the author.*

Lamson's built and occupied its luxurious palace-like store on Huron and Erie Streets. In the course of all these dramatic developments, the Lion Store was content to remain, homelike and welcoming to the customer base it had built for itself. The bulk of the store's space was located in buildings on St. Clair and Adams Streets, but the front door and the address remained with the lions at 329 Summit Street. Though it was necessary to cross an alley to connect from one store to another at the street-floor level, the upper levels were joined in such a way that patrons were generally unaware that they had passed from one building to another, making best use of the space available to the store.

On November 2, 1928, just a few days before the formal opening of Lamson's new store, the Lion Store announced to the press that it had purchased several properties on St. Clair Street and would demolish these buildings to build what the *Toledo News-Bee* referred to as "one of the largest downtown business property deals in recent years." The event marking the announcement was the Lion Store's acquisition of the Blade Printing and Paper Company Building at 320–24 St. Clair Street. This purchase completed the store's pursuit of property adjacent to its St. Clair Street building. Previously, the store bought the Hoffman Fur Building, a two-story, ornately detailed structure at 330 St. Clair Street and the venerable Tavern Hotel, which occupied the lot at 326–28 St. Clair.

The Tavern Hotel was originally built for the *Toledo Bee* in the 1890s in a Richardsonian Romanesque style with a façade of rough-hewn sandstone punctuated by a two-story bow window and crowned by a gable. When the *Toledo Bee* merged with the *Toledo News* in 1903 and no longer needed the building, it was converted to a hotel that catered mainly to theatrical personnel, owing to its proximity to the many theaters on St. Clair Street.

The two-story Hoffman Fur Building was also originally built for the *Toledo Bee* newspaper in 1900 and had as its distinguishing feature a neo-Renaissance bas-relief frieze above the second-floor windows. The building was converted to commercial use after being vacated by the *Bee* with an altered street floor that housed Hulce's Underwear & Hosiery shop at the time of the Lion Store's purchase of the premises.

The Blade Printing and Paper Company Building was a five-story, brick- and stone-faced commercial-style structure. The first floor housed the retail stationery and printing shop while offices and printing workshops were on the upper floors. With the acquisition of this building, the Lion Store attained a presence of 480 feet along St. Clair Street, and the 1928 announcement detailed plans for a physical plant that would put the Lion Store's operation on par with the large modern stores recently occupied by Lasalle's and Lamson's. It was noted, though, that the project could not start until the Blade Printing and Paper Company's lease expired in 1929.

The Lion Store's 1928 announcement outlined plans that would give Toledo "an institution rivaling any of its kind in the United States" and place the Lion Store "in the front rank in the matter of area, merchandising and service facilities, making it equal to almost any institution of its kind in this part of the country." Specifically, the plan envisioned adding stories to the newest parts of the store on St. Clair and Adams Streets and demolishing the newly acquired buildings on St. Clair Street, as well as the so-called

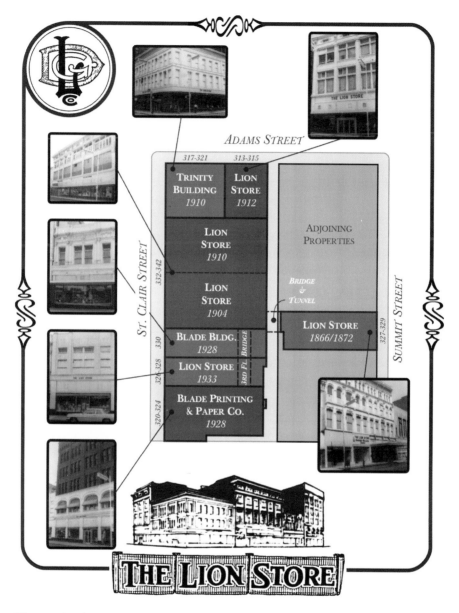

Diagram showing the location and opening or acquisition date of the Lion Store's disparate collection of buildings. *Artwork by the author.*

Trinity Building on the corner of St. Clair and Adams. These portions would be built out to match the augmented newer sections, giving the store a homogenous appearance on St. Clair Street and greatly increased space in which to do business. The Summit Street store would be integrated into the complex and improved as well.

It was not to be, however. The stock market crash of October 1929 seriously affected business in Toledo, and retailers struggled to survive. The Lion Store put its building plans on hold, eventually choosing to replace the Tavern Hotel building with a plain, modern, two-story brick-faced structure to connect the rest of its buildings to the Blade Printing edifice. A sloping, enclosed bridge "flew" over the two-story portions of the Lion Store to connect the former Blade Printing building to the 1904 portion of the Lion Store at the third-floor level. Years later, an advertising department employee joked to the *Blade* that she could easily roll her chair down the sloping floor of the bridge in order to visit nearby coworkers' desks. The announcement, in April 1933, of the opening and expansion of the enlarged store was terse and to the point without any of the fanfare and celebration that accompanied the predepression openings of the Lasalle and Lamson facilities.

Another development, which commenced before the onset of the Great Depression, was finished before economic difficulties put it on hold. In October 1928, the store opened a warehouse, garage and delivery center on the northern side of Downtown Toledo, where St. Clair and Superior Streets intersected. An existing building was renovated for the warehouse while the new garage and delivery center, with loading bays for the Lion Store's local delivery trucks, were erected adjacent to it. Newspapers touted the advancements that the facilities would bring to the store's operation as well as their ability to ease traffic congestion on St. Clair Street in the shopping district.

As the economic depression carried on through the 1930s and America entered World War II, the Lion Store settled in to its decidedly down-to-earth facilities, which, though they stood in contrast to competitors' larger and more impressive buildings, had a welcoming simplicity and smaller scale that, in the end, pleased customers and welcomed them back time and again. With the increased space, the store added a popular restaurant named the Coral Room to the first floor of the Summit Street building, which also received an elaborate entrance arcade with a free-standing, glass-enclosed showcase that sheltered arriving and departing customers from the weather and greatly increased the presence of display windows on Summit Street.

In the postwar era, the Lion Store assumed the role of one of Toledo's most popular and best-managed department stores. It was not the most exclusive and certainly not the largest, but its down-to-earth style, friendliness and policy of bringing value to its customers assured its success. When reminiscing about the Lion Store, Jamie Farr simply stated:

> *Everyone—and I mean anyone who grew up in Toledo—sat on the lions. We'd take a bus downtown, though it wasn't just* [for] *shopping. You didn't have to go downtown to buy something; it was fun just to go through the stores. Often, we'd take in a double-feature (with a newsreel, too!) at one of the cinemas—usually a Bette Davis film, one of my favorites. There was a terrific restaurant across the street from the Lion Store called Williams' Cafeteria. It was one of those places where your coffee came with half-and-half in little individual glass bottles, and the food was always remarkably good—a real treat. We'd have a quick lunch,* [and] *then go outside, where there were these beautifully decorated windows, which at the holidays were like giant greeting cards for everyone to gaze at. The imagination and beauty of these displays—and there wasn't just one but whole streets of them—celebrated the season and drew us in, right inside places* [such as] *the Lion Store. Of course, sitting on the lions was a part of the ritual for a child. It was an era when shopping was fun because there was a personal touch involved. In many ways, stores like the Lion Store reached out to* [people] *and became a part of their family.*

Employees of the Lion Store often remarked that the store's friendly and homelike atmosphere was one of its most endearing characteristics, citing the many downtown workers who visited on their lunch hours not just to browse but also to chat or wave "Hi" to salespeople they had known over the years. Other store employees commented that one of the store's great qualities was its range of merchandise, which was such that a customer could buy an aluminum ladder in the store's basement housewares section and come back for a bridal dress just a few floors up if need be.

The store's frequent sales included a highly awaited September "Anniversary Sale," and its special events were small-scaled, such as the store's contest that Toledo-born Wisconsin resident Sarah Hogoboom recalled: "My aunt sent me a clipping announcing that she and her friends from the Toledo Yacht Club won first prize in a Lion Store table-setting contest, probably sometime in the 1930s."

One of the Lion Store's great leaders at the time was Arthur J. Pete, who served as president for a remarkable twenty-six years. A native of Port Clinton, Ohio, he joined the Lion Store's staff in 1917 after gaining retail experience on Saturdays and after school during his youth. At the Lion Store, he began as a salesman in the phonograph department, which he built into a huge success. Eventually, he was made manager and, later, assumed the presidency, where he presided over good times and bad but always showed both compassion and leadership.

His grandson, Brent Bissel, offers an insight into his grandfather's longevity at the venerable Toledo store:

> *That period saw deft management during labor disputes through empowerment of the individual. I can remember the family story of my grandfather losing plenty of sleep during one such period, which he countered by being there through pretty much all the shifts and personally walking the store, getting to know each individual employee and their circumstances. My grandfather was without pretense, having been self-taught with only a high school formal education. The way they used to grow in position was through demonstrated integrity, employee empathy and motivation through knowledge of each person as a person.*

His comments are reinforced by his cousin's daughter, Stephany Anderson, who guards a tattered scrapbook given to Arthur Pete by employees on the occasion of his retirement in 1954. Inside the album, which was compiled and hand-decorated by an employee, are numerous letters and telegrams from current and former employees, business associates and even one from cosmetics magnate Elizabeth Arden. What connects them all are the unfailing appreciation and admiration expressed for Arthur Pete's character from a variety of people in many different walks of life.

A common thread running through the letters is illustrated by this one excerpt, which was written by Irving B. Cohen of Mercantile Stores Company:

> *I know you can look back at your life-long career at the Lion Store with the greatest pride of accomplishment. I do not believe there is another person associated with the Mercantile Stores who has made the consistent contribution to the company's success that you have. You have developed more store managers than any other individual in the company. You have likewise developed more merchandise managers. You have brought the Lion Store to a position of great respect in Toledo, by virtue of your own dynamic personality. You have inspired*

Retiring Lion Store president Arthur Pete and his wife, Goldie, read telegrams at a 1954 celebration honoring his appointment to chairman of the board. *Courtesy of Stephany Anderson.*

and stimulated everyone who has ever worked with you, to learn and love the excitement and intrigue of department-store life. The success you enjoyed in steadily building sales volume and earnings at the Lion Store is recognized as a real achievement and a personal triumph. I congratulate you on your achievements, on the affection your associates have for you and on the deep respect with which everyone in and out of business regards you.

Brent Bissel is fond of his memories of Arthur Pete's car. He says that his grandfather was "so integrated with the store" that, even after his retirement, his 1959 Ford Thunderbird sported a color scheme matching the store's shopping bags, "white above and Lion Store green below!" He also says that: "I have most pleasant memories of visiting the various stores and having the many employees swarm to say hello years after his (forced at the time) retirement." Arthur Pete retired as president of the

Lion Store after refusing a transfer to the New York corporate offices of Mercantile Stores.

The well-respected Pete was succeeded by another Mercantile Stores executive, J. Donald Ross, who was transferred from the chain's Castner-Knott Company store in Nashville, Tennessee. When Ross retired in 1962, he was followed by another Mercantile executive who was being groomed for the job, Leon Winbigler; likewise, he stayed with the store until the late 1960s, before assuming the presidency of Mercantile Stores Company itself. Even though Mercantile's leadership choices after Pete's retirement were not Toledo natives, these newcomers did involve themselves in the community's affairs in such a way that the store was primarily perceived by the Toledo public as a local institution.

In the prewar period and under Arthur J. Pete's leadership, the Lion Store reached its final form downtown. It was also poised to take the success it found in Downtown Toledo to markets outside the city, which, after the cessation of hostilities in 1945, was ready to grow along with the economic and population boom that loomed just over the horizon.

Lion Tales

Even during the war, the Lion Store sought to spread out beyond Downtown Toledo. Like many stores, the Lion Store took the first steps toward branch development tentatively, opening an appliance and home furnishings store in Bowling Green, Ohio, the seat of Wood County, located about twenty-four miles south of the main store. The branch opened in May 1944, clearly anticipating the pent-up demand for new home technologies that would inevitably occur after the end of World War II. Records have not survived, but the store must have been a success because it led to the opening, in 1945, of a companion store offering fashion apparel across the street in existing premises at 110 North Main Street.

Another development spreading the Lion Store's influence across northwestern Ohio occurred in November 1950, when, after the rehabilitation of the former Bond Furniture store at 219 Front Street, a three-story branch was established in Fremont, Ohio. Roughly thirty-seven miles southeast of Toledo, Fremont was once home to the nineteenth U.S. president, Rutherford B. Hayes. The city, seat of Sandusky County, was characterized by a popular downtown-shopping district that seemed ideal for the development of a modern department store.

The existing building was equipped with a new storefront and upgraded mechanical facilities before opening its doors as the Lion Store on November 14, 1950, though a formal grand opening did not occur until twelve days later. On the date of the event, the store thanked the city for its "wonderful and heartwarming" welcome and took its place as a major retail force on

The old buildings housing the Lion Store soldiered on as a shopping destination into the 1970s. *Ted Ligibel photo used by permission of the Toledo-Lucas County Library.*

Above: Fremont's Lion store opened in 1950 on Front Street, occupying a former furniture store renovated to the Toledo retailer's specifications. *Collection of the author.*

Opposite: Charming ad preparing Lion Store customers for Westgate's grand opening. *Collection of the author.*

Front Street, a fact that was reinforced by the two large signs—one on the new building canopy, and one overhanging the sidewalk vertically—that spelled out the store's name.

While not large by standards of later stores, the store was able to offer a full range of merchandise, as described in the *Fremont News-Messenger* at the time of the opening. The first floor offered yard goods, fashion accessories and a complete men's and boys' store to the shopping public in Fremont while the upper floors housed fashion departments and a beauty salon on the second and home furnishings and appliances on the third.

It was not until later in the decade that the Lion Store felt it necessary to expand in Toledo proper. That opportunity came when the Westgate Shopping Center was developed in the vicinity of Central and Secor Avenues west of downtown. The shopping center, which was the fourth to be developed in Toledo (after Miracle Mile, Great Eastern and Parkway Plaza), was developed by Bernard Greenabum of Chicago and was laid out on two sides of Central Avenue on the western side of Toledo. The grand opening of the center occurred on May 15, 1957, but the 100,000-square-foot Lion Store didn't itself open until August 15 of that year, signaling completion of the first phase of the large shopping center, which became the major

'just about SET to go!

Can't keep it under our hats any longer!
All the hustle and bustle you've
noticed at Lion Westgate
means we're just about ready
for company!
The last nail has been nailed, the farthest
corner painted, the chandeliers set in
place, the ultra—modern equipment
moved in . . . the brushes and hammers
have been packed, the sawdust all
swept up . . . we've waved goodbye
to the carpenters, plumbers, painters,
electricians and movers . . .
the carpets have been rolled in,
put down, and now we're
scurrying around with
dusters and mops making sure
that we'll be spic
and sparkling from top to bottom!
Such a flurry of polishing and scrubbing! . . .
shining the windows, vacuuming the carpets,
even giving our "Centennial
Coffee Bar" silver
an initial furbish (wait till
you taste our fragrant, freshly
brewed coffee).
Everyone's been trying the smooth
rides on our escalators . . .
enjoying the delightful coolness of
our new air conditioning . . . exclaiming
over the fine woods and pastel
colors used everywhere!
We've even heard YOU oh-ing and
ah-ing about the lush draperies that cover
our 200 feet of window display space!
Our staff is whirling
with excitement, jostling one
another, getting underfoot, bringing
in armloads of fresh, new
merchandise, filling the shelves,
dressing the mannequins (they can hardly
wait to show you all the lovely
things they have!)
Yes, we're all as busy as we can be,
doing all the last minute things that need
doing . . . and enjoying every exciting
minute of it. Even our Westgate Lion
(you can see him prancing for joy from afar)
is purring busily—he's counting the days
till we throw open the doors,
sweep off the sidewalks and
invite you all in (Be sure to
watch the papers for this event)
It won't be long now!

Lion WESTGATE

CENTRAL AT SECOR

You'll SHOP at Westgate because you like NICE things!

suburban retail destination in Toledo until the advent of Franklin Park Mall in 1971. Though the Lion Store did operate a garden center at Westgate prior to opening the main store, it apologized to customers that its store wasn't ready for the May festivities but predicted that its "largest and finest suburban department store" would become "Toledo's pacesetter for casual shopping" when it opened in a few months.

When it did open, the Lion Store's Westgate branch was the highlight of the store's hundredth-anniversary celebrations. Roughly similar in concept to the popular Lamson's Parkway Plaza store, the new Lion Store was almost three times as large, spreading across two levels and incorporating a restaurant on its second floor named the "Centennial Room." The modernistic, blocklike building sat at the intersection of both wings of the shopping center, which housed popular stores such as National Foods, S.S. Kresge, Mark Klaus and Doubleday Books. In fact, the tenant mix of the center was much more cosmopolitan and varied than might be the case today; even out-of-town stores such as Detroit's Sallan Jewelers and the well-known Chandler Shoe Salon tested new markets at Westgate.

The Lion Store announced the gala opening in a full-page ad that promised hourly door prizes and described the store:

> *Tomorrow…you'll see the fulfillment of a suburban dream…Lion Westgate…the most complete, most breathtaking suburban store in northwest Ohio! A masterpiece of architecture, with modern lighting, air conditioning, soft music. There's spaciousness inside out, from the huge 3,000-car parking lot to the wide aisles and roomy departments on both of two levels. Every bit of it is designed for your comfort, convenience and pleasure while shopping. You'll find a thrilling assortment of new merchandise for every phase of your daily life, for your home, for your family. Lion Westgate is the store with a future in mind—your future!*

The gala itself featured singer Denise Lor, "famed star of TV's Gary Moore show," and "pretty Bernice Rockwood, well-known song stylist," who were to be accompanied by the Royal Commanders Band.

The *Toledo Blade* noted some of the architectural features of the store, such as its pastel interior colors, but especially praised the two hundred feet of display windows with a transparent background that allowed passersby to see into the store, which it described as having a "modern motif." One interesting omission was the lack of lions at the entrance of the store, as had been traditional downtown. Perhaps it was because the store's logo now

The Lion Store promoted its new Westgate branch as "Toledo's most beautiful suburban store." *Collection of the author.*

incorporated a lion graphic into its design or that the store's association with the downtown lions were so much a part of its history for so many years that they were taken for granted.

Notwithstanding, the Lion Westgate became a great success, as did the shopping center. The second-phase parcel north of Central Avenue was developed to accommodate a freestanding Sears, opened in 1961, and the first Toledo branch of Lasalle's, which came along a year later. The Lion Store was expanded to incorporate a third floor just three years after its opening, in 1960. The new floor was primarily devoted to an expanded offering of house furnishings of various sorts, and a full-page ad in the *Blade* listed these as well as remodeled and expanded shops on the other two floors. An interesting feature of the third floor was a lounge area called the "Patio," which was described in

The Lion Store responded to downtown competition, even from its own stores, by undertaking a thorough remodeling in 1962. *Collection of the author.*

ORE PRESENTS AN ENTIRELY

New Look

DOWNTOWN

Because You've Always Liked to Shop at Lion . . .

We "take our customers to heart." We cherish our 105 years of friendship with Toledo (a record of service without equal in the city.) So naturally we want to make the time you spend with us a matter of pleasure as well as value. Paying compliments with an all new, modern decor featuring fascinating new colors, new floor covering, the finest lighting, the latest equipment, and more convenient department arrangement—this is our way. Behind the Lion Stores **New Look** stand the same integrity, the same excellence of merchandise, the Lion Store's same "homey" atmosphere as always. Really, you'll recognize us, all right, even in our grand **New Look!**

Do Come In—We Can't Wait to Show You . . .

If you haven't already taken the new escalator between our First and Second Floors, you'll want to now! It glides milady from one fashion-center to another. (Elevators and stairways will continue to serve all four floors, of course.) Most departments on the First Floor are relocated for your shopping convenience. For instance, men, all your wardrobe needs take up a one-stop area on Adams Street. Ladies, all accessories form a fashion-cluster in the heart of the store. Although not yet completed, Notions and the Closet Shop occupy a new position next to Fabrics—and both face St. Clair Street. Major Appliances are displayed on the Summit Street side.

Possibly the Greatest Change of All . . .

is our beautiful Fashion Second Floor with new spacious aisles providing plenty of room for browsing in the novel arrangements of departments. Come enjoy the completely new atmosphere of our Fashion Dress Department — and here's wonderful news — we've a new Bridal Shop and Formal Salon for your memorable moments. You'll now find sportswear near the elevators . . . Millinery, Shoes, Coats, and Furs with new positions too. The fresh, bright decor has been planned to make your fashion shopping the most pleasant in Downtown Toledo! And we know you'll be pleased with our gracious new Ladies' Lounge located across from the beautiful, new Beauty Salon.

Watch Us for Even More to Come Later On!

Continuous Modelling and Fashion Shows all Week . . .

See our exciting Fashion Show to be staged on our new First and Second Floor via our New Escalator. Living models wearing new Fall and Winter Fashions selected from our fabulous fashions arriving daily.

Shows at 11:30 a.m., 12:30 p.m., 1:30 p.m., 3 p.m., 7 p.m. and 7:30 p.m. Monday and Thursday.

Tuesday, Wednesday, Friday and Saturday shows at 11:30 a.m., 12:30 p.m., 1:30 p.m. and 3 p.m.

Organ Music Will Accompany all Shows!

Baldwin Organ Courtesy Great Lakes Piano Company

Lion

DOWNTOWN

the opening day ad: "As you step off the convenient escalator, you'll note the magnificent iron grilled doors which once graced a formal garden in Spain. Companion decorative accents—antique garden benches and handsome urns—suggest moments of leisure during your shopping there."

The new floor expanded the store to 150,000 square feet, but it apparently was still not enough to handle the traffic. In 1963, the store undertook an expansion that added a three-story building at the rear of the store, which added another 36,000 square feet of space to the popular branch.

Before the Lion Westgate store reached its ultimate size, changes were underway downtown as well. Encouraged by the success of the Westgate branch, the Lion Store announced a major remodeling of the aging downtown location. Leon Winbigler, president of the store, stated that the store had "confidence in the downtown area" and that "naturally, [it] would not put this money [estimated at a half-million dollars] in and then move out." Clearly, the comments were in response to fears that the new suburban developments and the arrival in Toledo of discount retailers cast a shadow on the future of downtown. Nonetheless, the Lion Store invested in the future of its physical plant, parts of which were over ninety years old. The announcement also noted the fact that many innovations introduced at Westgate would be incorporated in the downtown store and that both the conveniences and emphasis on fashion retailing would be "similar to Lion's Westgate operation."

Five months later, on November 2, the Lion Store was ready to present the newly remodeled flagship to the public but not before the Downtown Toledo Associated recognized the retailer's contributions to the downtown district with the unveiling of a commemorative plaque. The remodeled store featured a relocated men's store inside the Adams Street entrance, escalators to the second-floor fashion departments and a new restaurant called the "Copper Lantern" in the former Hoffman Fur Building. The store's yard goods, luggage, book and stationery departments were located to the south of the new eatery in the 1933 annex and former Blade Printing Building.

The most notable changes were incorporated on the store's second floor, where newly redesigned and relocated sections sold fashion apparel for women and children. A new and expanded beauty salon with an adjacent ladies' lounge was a major feature. Throughout November 1962, the Lion Store's ads touted the "New Look" given the store and quoted Greek philosophers Plato and Socrates when describing the benefits to customers brought on by the renewal. Six months after the interior was completed, a new marquee was installed along Adams Street, and part of the Summit

Street frontage and display windows were renewed. A large mosaic logo replaced a display window next to the main entrance on St. Clair Street, which was located in the part of the building opened in 1910.

The Summit Street building, once the store's "front door" but now relegated to annex status, was remodeled in 1968, in a plain, somewhat uninviting manner. Of course, the lions remained outside, but a blank tiled storefront now greeted customers where the lavish display window alcove arrangement once welcomed Summit Street shoppers. Large plain letters spelled out "LION" over the doors that led to the store's appliance and TV department. With the relocation and replacement of the Coral Room restaurant, space for a paint department and a tenant lease with an entrance on Summit Street was gained, but before long, Summit Street's decline and ultimate destruction in favor of an urban-renewal program that would drastically alter its character loomed over the horizon.

Further suburban store development had to wait until the 1970s. In fact, in 1963, the Fremont and Bowling Green stores closed, no doubt victims of peripheral retail development on the fringes of the small towns they inhabited. Another factor that played against these downtown branch stores was the lack of traffic in their central business districts due to the new expressways that allowed cars to roar past the towns, the Ohio Turnpike in the case of Fremont and the north–south Interstate 75 for Bowling Green. Ultimately, customers in these smaller towns preferred the newly proliferated shopping plazas near expressway exits with their discount stores and parking lots, forcing not just local merchants but also large out-of-town competitors such as the Lion Store to reevaluate their presence on the historic downtown streets that had once formed a shopping, dining and entertainment nucleus.

The Lion Store was content through most of the 1960s to operate as a two-unit chain, but as the decade came to a close, the big news was Southwyck, the shopping component of a planned community named Hawthorn Hills, developed jointly by the Lion Store and the Bailey Company of Kansas City. An agreement between these parties, in which the Lion Store would own and develop the retail portion of the community on Reynolds Road near the Ohio Turnpike, was announced in early 1968. Construction did not begin, however, for a number of years due to a variety of legal issues, leaving Southwyck to open in 1972, over a year after Franklin Park Mall established itself as a major shopping destination.

The opening, though, was a grand affair, with longtime Metropolitan Opera bass Giorgio Tozzi singing the national anthem. While the brick-and-concrete Lion Store's large size (190,000 square feet) was noted by local

The Southwyck store was the largest suburban Lion Store in the 1970s. *Collection of the author.*

newspapers, the store, with deeply recessed arcades along its perimeter, offered merchandising style and dimension that surpassed the its successful Westgate presentation and was simply not possible in the downtown store's constricted environment. The store's ads invited Toledoans to come see "a modern masterpiece of shopping convenience and spacious beauty! Lion presents northwest Ohio's largest, most unique fashion department store...dazzling in every detail of color combinations, shapes, textures, designs, blending in tasteful contemporary elegance. Wide aisles beckon you to explore the vast spectrum of exciting name fashions and home furnishings...For the first time in Toledo, see the fast and fascinating computerized handling of your sales transactions!"

The store printed a series of ads showing sketches that featured the unique and contemporary merchandising style adopted by the store's designers and promised merchandise of a decidedly upscale nature in the store's many boutique-like shops. The use of plush carpets and natural woods was mentioned, along with the latest in lighting techniques, creating a "breath-taking atmosphere of rare luxury." The ads may have been heavy in hyperbole, but it was an undisputed fact that the Lion Store trumped its hometown competition with a store that was a fairly dramatic departure from the style of its predecessors.

Toledo's Greatest Store

The Lasalle & Koch Company, known to generations of Toledoans as "Lasalle & Koch's," (the latter name is pronounced "Cook's"), wasn't the oldest store in Toledo. While it was a fashionable place, described by Jamie Farr as "smacking of money and high-end good taste," it wasn't the most exclusive department store in the city, either. Those roles were taken by the Lion Store and Lamson's, respectively. What Lasalle's was, however, was just what one of its slogans implied: "Toledo's Greatest Store." It was the largest, most universal and prominent department store in the city, and it was the retailer most thoroughly identified with Toledo. Though it ceased to be locally owned fifty-eight years into its history, when the great R.H. Macy & Company of New York City acquired an interest in it, Lasalle's remained deeply rooted in Toledo and tossed off its out-of-town relationship with Macy's by reminding customers that Toledo's Greatest Store "was only five minutes from New York."

Lasalle's became the retailer most beloved by Toledoans in spite of its humble beginnings and later associations with New York. It was the only one of Toledo's department stores that could have been placed in a city twice Toledo's size and still seem entirely at home. The building in which it was housed could rival any other store of the era for the beauty and monumentality of its architecture and appointments. Lamson's built itself a jewel-like Florentine palazzo, and the Lion Store developed a unique, down-to-earth atmosphere in its odd collection of buildings; but Lasalle's went over the top with its grand establishment, artfully composed of brick and stone. It was cosmopolitan, and its status as a downtown anchor is proven by the fact that, as it grew and relocated, the city expanded and moved to meet it, wherever it went.

Father Justin DuVall is archabbot of St. Meinrad's Archabbey in southern Indiana. Born in Toledo, Abbot Justin lost his biological mother at age three, and his stepmother, Nancy DuVall, whom he refers to as "the only mother I really ever knew," worked at Lasalle's. As a young man, the future Benedictine priest had the privilege of going to work with his mom on school snow days and duly got to know the downtown store: "It was so big to a little kid. On those days with my mom downtown, I'd just sit on a chair in the better coat department, where she worked. I got to know her colleagues and even her boss." He goes on about his experiences with Lasalle's: "The enormous store held the world in it, and it stimulated my imagination. To a young child, it was a fascinating and mysterious environment. My mother would take me to the eighth floor, where we'd have a sit-down lunch. One thing that was certain was that, while there, I had to be on my best manners, no matter what. You might think that made it stuffy or unpleasant, but it is a memory I cherish, and an atmosphere which just doesn't exist today."

Likewise, actor Jamie Farr relishes memories of his favorite hometown store, Lasalle's: "Well, first of all, it had a great men's department, and especially at Christmas, it was a real experience to go there. The store was decorated beautifully. We browsed but rarely bought on the first, second or third floors—the basement was more appropriate to our budget. But when they had sales, you could get a bargain, and you felt so good about it. The people there really waited on you and made you feel like a valued customer." The renowned actor adds a philosophical viewpoint to his memories, however, stating:

> *It was perhaps not just the store, but that very time in people's lives that made it so special. We lived fairly simple lives, but the very thought of going to that magnificent place to shop took us on a journey, full of excitement and imagination. It truly is an era long gone. You knew where your shoes were made, how to recognize fine woolens or that the best in furniture came from North Carolina. The department stores had all of those great trademarks, and the store's name alone was a further assurance of quality. So, people dressed in their best to go there, in anticipation of the service they'd receive. Lasalle & Koch's, as we knew it then, was even a little snobbish on the upper floors, but we didn't mind because it was an indication of the class and quality that the store had.*

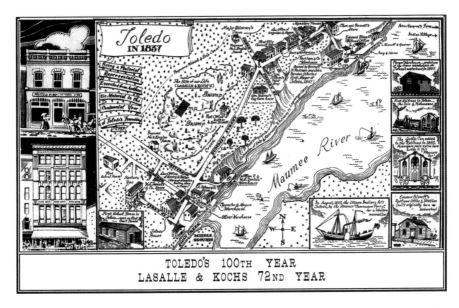

In 1937, Lasalle's published illustrations of Toledo at its founding and of its earliest stores in 1865, *top left*, and 1883, *bottom left*. *Collection of the author.*

Before it grew into the institution that called itself "Toledo's Greatest Store," the Lasalle & Koch Company had humble beginnings. Its founder, Jacob Lasalle, was born in 1833 in town of Marsberg, in the Prussian province of Westphalia, and immigrated to the United States as a young man after a year of service in the German army. He settled first in Dubuque, Iowa, and later in Milwaukee and Chicago, respectively. In each of these locations he took on a business venture, made a fortune and eventually lost it due to poor circumstances.

With the outbreak of Civil War in 1861, Lasalle formed a company of his peers, German-born Jews who wished to fight for the Union. This company was accepted into the Eighty-second Regiment Illinois Volunteer Infantry, the so-called "Second Hecker Regiment," a mostly German regiment of the Union army, which was named after Friedrich Hecker, its commander. Lasalle served as a captain for the duration of the war and fought, in what his obituary called later, "many hot engagements." After the cessation of hostilities, Lasalle married Miss Sybilla Stern, who remained with him for the rest of his life, and the couple moved to Toledo after a fairly intensive search for an ideal location to start a business.

On September 14, 1865, with a partner, Joseph Epstein, Lasalle leased a twenty- by sixty-foot space at 51 Summit Street and opened a dry goods business under the name of Lasalle & Epstein. Toledo of the day had a population of about twenty thousand people, and the retail business was concentrated along Summit Street.

Meanwhile, Joseph Koch, a native of Framersheim, Germany, in the Rhineland, immigrated to the United States at the age of sixteen in 1866 and made his home in Toledo. At the time, there was a dry goods store owned by J.W. Mullinix that was located on Summit near Monroe Street, not far from Jacob Lasalle's growing enterprise. Koch took a position as a clerk with Mullinix's store and, in two years, moved on to Frederick Eaton's Bee Hive, where he remained for nine years. Through his determination and ability to save, he was able to open the doors of his own dry goods firm in partnership with Alies S. Cohen in 1877.

Lasalle and Koch first came together in 1881, when Joseph Koch left the partnership with Cohen, who himself closed shop in 1883 and joined with Lasalle and Koch in business. The combined firm became known as Lasalle, Cohen and Koch until Cohen left the firm three years later to found the Cohen, Friedlander & Martin Company, a manufacturer of cloaks, which were sold under the trade name "Redfern." Joseph Koch married Hattie Black of Toledo in 1884, but after bearing him three children, she passed away in 1896. After his first wife's death, he remarried to her sister Belle, and the couple had two more offspring. The long-demolished Koch residence was located at 1937 Franklin Street.

From that time on, the name Lasalle & Koch Company was to be attached to a dynamic enterprise that was well on its way to becoming the retailer known as "Toledo's Greatest Store." The fledgling enterprise led by Jacob Lasalle and Joseph Koch was, early on, a family affair, including Lasalle's brother Sol and Koch's brother Abe as officers. The small, original shop was outgrown, and new premises on the southwestern corner of Summit and Adams became the home of a larger store in 1883. Years later, a Lasalle's anniversary ad proclaimed:

The little store showed the mettle which was to shape for it a destiny little dreamed of by its founders or the people of that day. It dug its roots into the soil of the city. It began to belong. It grew steadily, prospered, expanded. And at last it had to seek larger quarters…Meanwhile, Toledo was growing, industry was expanding, the march of scientific progress was in full beat. Firmly rooted in the tradition and the soil of the city, already an important community institution, the Lasalle & Koch Company matched strides with a marching Toledo.

True to these words, the store was forced to add three floors to the property at Summit and Adams to accommodate its growth. Interestingly, in this period, three of Toledo's major department stores were located cheek-by-jowl on one block, with Lamson Brothers next door to Lasalle & Koch's to the south, followed by the Lion Store just beyond it. It is also worthwhile to note that, like other Summit Street dry goods houses (among them the Thompson-Hudson Company, Mockett's, Neuhausel's and Milner's), Lasalle's sold primarily dress fabrics, cloaks, house furnishings and shoes since ready-to-wear apparel had not yet become popular by this time.

The Secor family of Toledo made its name in banking and real estate. Family patriarch and member of the Society of Friends Joseph Secor came to Toledo in the 1860s from Goshen, New York and, along with his philanthropist wife, Elizabeth, built a financial and property empire, which was carried on by their only surviving son, Arthur. Joseph's younger brother James followed him westward and took his place in the family's enterprises, as did his son Jay. One of the family's most dramatic contributions to Toledo was the gorgeous, representative Secor Hotel, built in 1908 at 435 Jefferson Avenue.

Sixteen years earlier, however, catty-corner from the future site of their hotel, the Secors built a speculative building in a Renaissance Revival style with stone trim contrasting the brick that was used to sheath four of the building's six floors. The existing structure was later deemed ideal for Lasalle & Koch's needs, and in 1900, the store's advertisements told patrons: "We are moving to the corner of Jefferson and Superior Streets." A removal sale was advertised for quite some time, until on April 1, 1900, the store was able to hold a formal grand opening at the new location.

The announcement of the move, and its fulfillment, may have seemed unusual to both customers and competitors at the turn of the century. The new Lasalle & Koch location was two blocks west of Summit Street, then the city's dominant retail corridor, and several blocks south of the proverbial "100 percent corner" of Summit and Adams where Lasalle & Koch's had been doing business for seventeen years. However, the firm had seriously outgrown its physical plant and the new location offered plenty of space and room in which to grow. The partners admitted later that they had to spread merchandise throughout the large new location in order to make it seem fully stocked, but the same anniversary ad referenced above gives an idea of the logic of the move from hindsight: "By 1900, the Lasalle & Koch Company was seeking a new and larger home. The next move was a daring one. In 1900 Lasalle & Koch's moved to the corner of Jefferson and Superior Streets. This was far from the popular shopping district and many timid souls predicted

The 1900 Lasalle & Koch store shown from the corner of Superior Street and Jefferson Avenue. The buildings to the rear are additions, dating from 1906 and 1908, respectively. *From the Business & Industry of Greater Toledo Collection, Toledo-Lucas County Public Library.*

disaster. But Toledo continued to grow, and Lasalle & Koch's with it. Twice were the premises enlarged to accommodate the steadily increasing patronage, and before long, the dream of a modern skyscraper home was forming."

Far from suffering disaster at Jefferson and Superior, the move solidified Lasalle's position as a forward-looking leader in the department store field. In terms of sheer space, the new store vied with Milner's as Toledo's largest, and its opening brought the shopping district westward with it. Lasalle & Koch's Summit Street competitors were suddenly left with small, older buildings that stood in contrast to the dynamic new Lasalle's. Six years after the move, the store grew by almost one half with the expansion of three bays (60 feet) to the north; in 1908, another two were added, extending the store a total of 170 feet down Superior Street. Just eight years after moving to the location that others thought problematic, Lasalle's occupied over 140,000 square feet of space and was doing better than ever.

During this time, Lasalle's began advertising itself as the "Style Store" since it could, through its greatly expanded stocks, act as a fashion arbiter to the Toledo shopper. In the same advertisements in which it exalted the last word in apparel and house furnishings from the world over, the Lasalle & Koch Company could, due to its size, hint at the fact that it was developing a position as Toledo's leading retailer.

On June 26, 1904, Joseph Koch passed away suddenly at the age of fifty-four. His death came after a period of suffering from a "disease of the throat" that was incorrectly not thought to be life threatening. His newspaper obituary recounted his "sheer determination to succeed" and the story of how he "fought his way upward" to become part owner and vice-president and general manager of the Lasalle & Koch Company. Newspapers reporting on his death noted that Koch was not of any particular religious affiliation, but the funeral service in his home was presided over by Rabbi Charles Freund of Toledo's Tenth Street Temple. Like many of Toledo's business and industrial greats, he was interred in the city's Woodlawn Temple.

One of Lasalle's employees at the time of Koch's death was Louis Eppstein, who, as a child, sold newspapers and shined shoes on Summit and Adams Streets. He came from an impoverished family—his father peddled secondhand goods in Toledo—and one day, Louis brazenly asked Koch to give him a job while polishing the storeowner's shoes. Koch obliged the young man but, learning that Louis didn't have a suit of clothing appropriate for work in a retail store, relegated him to odd outside jobs and deliveries. When he was able to save enough from his labor (and an after-hours career as an amateur boxer, earning two dollars per fight at St. Clair Street's Palace Theater), he bought a suit at Hudson's across the street (Lasalle's didn't carry men's clothing at the time) and was given a job in the store's wrapping department in 1877. His personal qualities were noticed by various department managers, and he grew through the organization.

Upon Joseph Koch's death in 1904, his son Alfred B. Koch left his studies at the University of Michigan and went to work for his late father's business. In due time, Eppstein and the younger Koch struck up a friendship. Later, Eppstein recalled, "Joseph Koch worked hard to help me. So naturally, I worked hard to help Alfred take his father's place." In fact, while Eppstein rose from poverty to work in the store, Koch came from privilege and found that the Lasalle's management worried that his sudden employment on the occasion of his father's death would amount to nothing more than nepotism.

JOSEPH KOCH
1850-1904

ALFRED B. KOCH
1884-1937

THE LASALLE & KOCH CO.

Father and son: Joseph and Alfred Koch. They both lived until their early fifties. *Collection of the author.*

According to Eppstein, the fears were unfounded: "He was a natural. We came to see that he was a natural, that he had leadership. So us older fellows stood aside, helped him all we could from our longer experience and watched him rise to the presidency of a great store which he made greater."

Indeed, the younger Koch quickly worked his way through various departments of the store and was appointed general manager of the Lasalle & Koch Company in 1911 and president ten years later. Of Alfred B. Koch it was said that the phenomenal growth of the store mirrored his own growth as an executive and as a civic leader. For the store, however, Koch's biggest achievement was to come, as Europe suffered the cataclysm of the Great War, and the United States itself became involved in the conflict.

More Than a Store, a Community Institution

If Alfred B. Koch's story is characterized by his leadership of an ascendant department store, a major pinnacle in his career became known to Toledoans when they read the *Blade* on Wednesday, August 2, 1916. On that day, standing out from news of the war raging in Europe, common gossip and tales of bribery in politics was an artist's conception of a monumental commercial building under the headline "New Home for Lasalle & Koch Co. Is To Be Erected at Adams and Huron." The article itself called the announcement "the biggest real estate deal of the year" and noted the building's proposed features, all to be enrobed in a structure distinguished by "Italian Renaissance architecture, this feeling being worked out clearly in the first two and the top two stories" with an interior composed of Travertine stone, "the material that has proved so ornamental in the Grand Central and Pennsylvania stations in New York City." The younger Koch was able to persuade Edward D. Libbey to finance the construction of the store, helping to make his dream a reality.

Alfred B. Koch made the announcement to the press, along with fellow executive Sol A. Lasalle. The *Blade* article indicated the basic arrangement of the eight-story emporium, with "various departments, dining rooms, grills, rest and recreation rooms, and other similar purposes." Noted also were the building's up-to-the-minute technical installations, which included a fur vault large enough to store $2 million in furs and an elevator bank arranged in an arc so that "customers can easily observe the operation of all cages." Detailed mention of the elevator's safety systems was also made, presumably a concern at the time, especially when installed in such a tall and capacious building. A practical feature of the store was the fact that its main floor would join with the existing Spitzer Arcade to the north to provide an enclosed pedestrian thoroughfare through both buildings from Adams to Madison Streets. (Later, when the connection became part of Toledoans' lives, they referred to it affectionately as "Lasalle Street.")

From the paragraphs of the article, one can almost see Alfred B. Koch's countenance beaming with pride as he described what the future held for the Lasalle & Koch Company and, of course, for Toledo's public as well: "The new store will be as modern, as up-to-date and as artistic as money can make it. We have spent months studying the problem and have sent men to cities all over the country to study the architecture and improvements in the most modern stores. We believe Toledo will be surprised and pleased with the results."

Koch's comments, notable for lacking the hyperbole that often characterized news of this magnitude, masked the fact that the new store had been a dream of his for some time; the buildings at Superior and Jefferson were a combination of additions to a structure built for a different purpose, and the retail trade, especially for department stores, was growing at a rate that made facilities that were state of the art when new quickly outdated by advances in store design.

Lasalle & Koch's choice of the New York firm of Starrett and van Vleck as architects is an indicator of just where its team looked to see the "most modern stores." The firm's principal was architect Goldwin Starrett, who worked for Daniel Burnham, whose firm designed Wanamaker's, Marshall Field & Company and Filene's, among other great stores. One of Starrett's first commissions after leaving the Burnham firm was the well-admired flagship of Newark's Hahne & Company, and his firm later garnered notice for the design of the large Kaufman & Baer (later Gimbels) department store in Pittsburgh. Until Lasalle's started looking for an architect, though, Starrett and van Vleck's most prominent and universally lauded department store creation was the new Fifth Avenue home of Lord & Taylor, which effortlessly and iconically housed one of America's oldest and most deluxe retailers. That the Lasalle & Koch management made the right choice was proven not only by the eventual results in Toledo but also by Starrett and van Vleck's continuing commissions for department store buildings, among them Saks Fifth Avenue (1924), Garfinckel's (Washington D.C., 1928) and a major 1930 addition to Bloomingdale's east side New York store, executed in a forward-looking art deco style.

First in a series of ads announcing Lasalle & Koch's new store. *Collection of the author.*

Over the next fourteen months, Toledoans watched the colossus that was to become Lasalle & Koch rise over the corner of Adams and Huron. When it took form and its details were revealed from behind scaffolding, the qualities of the structure showed themselves to be remarkable not just in size but also in their beauty and integrity of detail and composition. These characteristics had the power to make the building come alive on a human scale and immediately gave the building the status of a landmark. The building, too, by its very nature, associated the Lasalle & Koch Company with the desirable aspects of permanence, integrity and quality that it so clearly embodied.

As opening day approached, Lasalle & Koch's busied itself with closeout sales in the old store, informing customers, "We are extremely anxious not to take over to our new store, a single item of present stock." The company also took out a series of full-page ads in Toledo newspapers to introduce its new home to the shopping public. Essentially public service announcements, the ads served to portray the future of Lasalle's as it was to be expressed in the great building, while it was being prepared for opening day. Works of art in themselves, these ads were stylistic and beautifully illustrated, and their words, more like fine literature than advertising, betrayed the passion with which the retailer viewed its soon-to-be opened new home.

An ad entitled "The Tissue of Dreams" showed a partial image of the Lasalle & Koch store coming down, as if from the heavens, on swirling clouds with a female figure reclining nearby. Her hand shades her eyes as she gazes at the store, emphasizing the brilliance of the new creation that Lasalle's, its architects and its builders conceived. The wording, as in each of the ads, transcends mere advertising script and takes on a poetic tone:

After all the long days and nights—after all the effort of hand and heart and brain—next Tuesday morning we shall dedicate to your use our new home. Imagination wove a canvas and painted a picture, an ideal. It is now about to face the reality—the result of its handicraft—the dream-of-dreams will have come true. The splendid edifice and all that it contains will be ready to serve you. And as we look upon its graceful lines—the finely wrought and chiseled features which serve but to conceal its rugged strength—we realize what pleasure is—we have dreamed dreams—and made them come true. "We have done good work." Therefore, it is our sincerest wish that this, our New Home—with its conveniences, its merchandise, its service possibilities—may bring you, all shoppers of Toledo and vicinity, as much pleasure in its use as it has given us in producing it for such a splendid purpose.

For all its craft, the ad was merely an introduction, for daily afterward, new ones followed that touched on one aspect of the new edifice after another. The next ad, entitled "The Reality," showed a sketch of the new Lasalle & Koch's with automobiles and streetcars whizzing by, the store itself rooted in terra firma. The story, as told, continued:

> *Now we face the reality. The splendid edifice is here to speak for itself. Its wondrous beauty tells the story of a loving hand that has been wrought well. We see how Beauty has been made to serve Utility; we learn how it hides any and all merchandising marvels of the age—it is a step in advance of anything that has gone before. It will be a store which is more perfect in its appointments than any in the largest cities simply because it is latest and is the last word in supplying human needs. This beautiful building with all its equipment is now ours—in a few days, it will be yours also, ready to minister mechanically and personally to your wants, your personal comforts and needs. In this respect, it has reduced shopping to an art. All of the wonderful equipment—exterior and interior, mechanical and personal—is here to serve you, whoever you are or wherever you are, that seek its services.*

The Toledo public of the day had for some time paid attention to the goings on at Adams and Huron: the clearing of old buildings, the great steel frame rising out of the ground and its being clad with neo-Renaissance dress until the whole thing was topped with a dramatic overhanging cornice. Yet it is doubtful that Toledoans of 1917 could conceive how a mere building could "reduce shopping to an art." These ads captured a unique, intangible moment of imagination and creation and gave rise to the question that was surely on the minds of Lasalle's future customers: "Just what could it be like inside?"

No amount of florid language or any attractive drawings could give an adequate answer to this question until the crowds themselves entered the Lasalle & Koch Company's new doors, but the ostentatious ads continued to appear each day, enticing customers further. Showing a detailed drawing of one of the new store's grandiose arched entrances and entitled "The New Era," another ad reassured Toledoans:

> *With the opening of our doors in this splendid edifice comes "The New Era." Not to us alone nor to our customers, but to the whole of Toledo and vicinity. The standard of living has been changed for every family that comes within its sphere of influence. The beautiful things of life, the material comforts and luxuries of life, will have touched Toledo and made the home life much more*

The second ad in the series, titled "The Reality," sang the praises of the new store. *Collectionof the author.*

worthwhile. Something of the joy of the worker in his work, something of the fine enthusiasm of the artist in creation, will have come into many more lives, thrilling them and touching a responsive chord. Our beautiful store in its beauty and the splendid things it contains has made Toledo different for you for all times hereafter. It is "The New Era."

One ad, entitled "Big Things," compared the vastness of the store to St. Paul's cathedral in London and St. Peter's in Rome while another, entitled "All's Well," forecast the pleasure with which the public would receive Lasalle & Koch's huge investment. Prior to a lavishly illustrated ad inviting all of Toledo to come to the store's grand opening, one more document in the series, under the heading "Brass Tacks," explained why Lasalle's advertised no merchandise or sales over the week prior to the opening and summarized what it hoped to accomplish on the corner of Adams and Huron Streets:

Something of what the dreaming, planning, and building of our new store has meant to us we have told you. We have stepped aside for a moment from the beaten path to visit with you that you might understand. Tomorrow the veil will be lifted—the Beautiful Building and all it contains becomes a public institution—tomorrow and forever afterward, it is yours to use and enjoy; it is the utility phase, the getting down to "Brass Tacks." It is therefore, peculiarly fitting to repeat here, the principles for which we stand, those splendid ideals crystalized out of the best in modern business methods, the spirit of which imbues our every employee from least to greatest. Regarding Merchandise: That all merchandise shall be of the dependable kind and sold as such without exaggeration. Regarding Service: That each transaction shall be satisfactory from beginning to end, without discrimination. Regarding Errors: That we shall cultivate a readiness to rectify errors cheerfully, with a constant effort to eliminate them. Regarding Courtesy: That we shall treat every customer, regardless of circumstances, with unfailing courtesy, approaching our work with a spirit of helpfulness and willingness to spend and be spent in your service.

The heartfelt optimism conveyed in this series of advertisements was reflective not only of a proud and growing business but also of a city and an era, which, in spite of an ongoing war, looked confidently toward a future built on increasing wealth and a belief that progress could solve any problems a city or nation might face. The Lasalle & Koch Company, because it saw itself as an indivisible part of the city of Toledo, and indeed of America

THE NEW ERA

WITH the opening of our doors in this splendid edifice comes "The New Era."–Not to us alone, nor to our customers, but to the whole of Toledo and vicinity. The standard of living has been changed for every family that comes within its sphere of influence. The beautiful things of life – the material comforts and luxuries of life will have touched Toledo and made the home-life much more worth while. Something of the joy of the worker in his work – something of the fine enthusiasm of the artist in creation, will have come into many more lives, thrilling them and touching a responsive chord. Our beautiful store in its beauty and the splendid things it contains has made Toledo different for you for all times hereafter. It is "The New Era."

The Lasalle & Koch Co.
ADAMS AND HURON STREETS

The third ad in the series illustrated one of the store's three arched entries. *Collection of the author.*

itself, willingly participated in the progress thought necessary to move the society in which it existed forward. With the construction of its new store, Lasalle's didn't just build a big box; it raised the bar of public expectations of what a store could be.

When the doors did open, at noon on Tuesday, November 13, 1917, about ninety thousand people poured through them to see Toledo's new temple of commerce. The store had "official counters" stationed at the door, and though they reached a tally of eighty-six thousand persons, the crowds swelled so much that the counting process was deemed impossible and had to be discontinued. Alfred B. Koch later noted plainly that the lack of confusion "surely attest[s] to the excellent facilities and the thoroughness which have been incorporated into our new home."

The store that the public saw on the occasion was much more than the fulfillment of what had been promised before, and newspaper reports describing it waxed almost as poetically as the store's pre-opening advertisements. The eight-story building filled a lot with a 120-foot frontage on Adams Street and 280 feet on Huron, adjacent to the existing Spitzer Building. One of the main characteristics of the new store was its main floor of incredible height—29 feet—which was reflected on the exterior by tall recessed limestone arcades along the street sides of the building. The arches, themselves formed of stone and carrying a decorative frieze above, were supported along the street sides of the structure by Doric columns of polished granite. Three of the component arches, one on Adams Street, and two on Huron street, formed the building's main entrances. These were more deeply recessed and housed monumental lantern-style light fixtures hung above the entrance doors. A fourth entrance to the building was incorporated from the Spitzer Building's arcade.

The remainder of the main floor's arches housed twenty show windows, which the *Toledo Blade* referred to as "no more or less than a series of crystal palaces." These vitrines projected out from the deeply recessed arcades and featured butt-glazed corners crowned by a delicately articulated decorative bronze parapet. Retractable awnings protected the store display and passersby from the sun, and a pair of bronze plaques at the Adams and Huron corner proudly announced the store's name. The remarkable composition of the building's elevations at street floor belied the bulk of the enormous department store within and gave the city of Toledo a lively, transparent and welcoming streetscape, which, as long as the building exists, must be considered a masterstroke in the annals of twentieth-century commercial architectural design.

The building's fundamental base was continued up past the frieze to the second floor, which was also sheathed in limestone and punctured by windows. The major bulk, or "shaft," of the classically inspired structure was covered in a deep chestnut-colored brick, whose monotony was relieved not just by

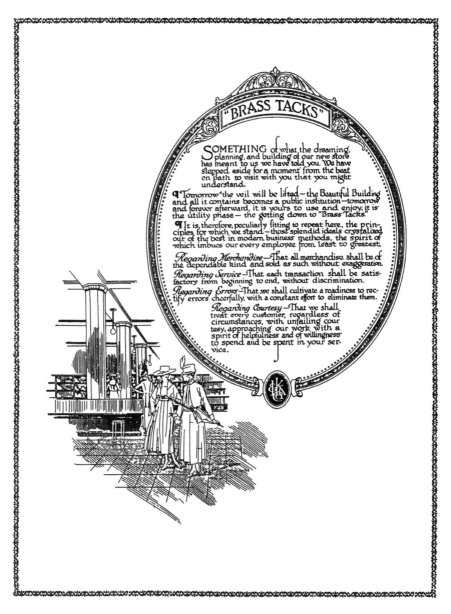

The "Brass Tacks" ad outlined the Lasalle & Koch Company's policies as a merchant. The 1917 store was revolutionary, and the business also had to rise up and meet what it represented to customers. *Collection of the author.*

the vast grid of windows but also by purposeful surface recesses and special brick corner detailing. Stone balconies, which have since been removed, projected on both façades from the fifth-floor level, from which sprouted enormous flagpoles, used for special occasions. All of this was capped by a two-story, loggia-like colonnade supporting a distinctly Mediterranean-looking parapet that extended far over the building's façades and allowed the marvelous composition itself to meet the sky in a majestic manner. In characterizing the store, the *Blade* emphasized that "the temptation to gaudy embellishment has been carefully withstood."

Inside, the effect of refined monumentality was no less prolific, as early photographs show. Reports of the day claimed that the store's decorative effect was inspired by the magnificent cathedral in Toledo's namesake town on the Iberian Peninsula, but any such relation was secondary to the sheer grandeur of the vast and lofty main floor, characterized by a forest of tall, octagonal columns that emerged from a sea of mahogany showcases with black stone bases and plate-glass tops and fronts. The wide aisles of travertine served not just to ease customer traffic but also to enforce the sense of space and perspective within the store, referred to by the *Blade* as a "cathedral-like" place "of admirable vistas and magnificent distances."

The walls of the main floor were likewise sheathed in travertine, and great decorative grills served to ventilate the space and add artistry to the composition of the walls at the same time. The elevators, laid out in a shallow arc as noted earlier, were located on the wall opposite the Huron Street side of the store, and their doorways were surmounted by lofty arches that reached almost to the great height of the ceiling. Each elevator's doors were beautifully cased in mahogany and bronze; the stone pilasters that framed the whole arrangement incorporated recessed decorative drinking fountains whose stone surrounds made them appear to be miniature roman temples—yet another aspect of this remarkable building that raised the mundane (such as taking a drink of water) into a work of art.

Above the glorious main floor were five floors dedicated to various types of merchandise, a seventh floor containing the store's offices and an eighth floor that housed a spacious auditorium and several restaurants, including a "Fountain Dining Room," "Loggia" and a "Men's Grill" that was "equipped with a French rotisserie of the latest sort where one can see his chop or his steak cooked after he has selected it himself." An employees' cafeteria and lounge room as well as a kitchen large enough to serve the floor's capacity of two thousand people were located on the eighth floor. Above, a ninth-floor

Above: The new Lasalle & Koch store shortly after opening in 1917. *By permission of the Toledo-Lucas County Library.*

Opposite: Lofty interior of the Lasalle & Koch store. The curved bank of elevators surmounted with decorative arches can be seen on the left. *By permission of the Toledo-Lucas County Library.*

penthouse led to a roof terrace "with space for tennis courts and handball, to say nothing of banquets and garden parties."

Although unseen by most of the store's patrons, the building's technical wonders were touted in advertisements and newspaper reports, from the fireproof stair towers to the technical details of the state-of-the art elevators. The store's water needs were supplied by a series of tanks on the roof, which later became something of a symbol for Lasalle & Koch's, and its massive heating plant, located in one of the store's four basements, was so large that the company sold steam heat to neighboring buildings for many years. Seemingly, no detail was left without consideration—even the eighth-floor kitchens were equipped with a mechanism that froze up to three thousand pounds of garbage a day "without ever attracting a single fly."

The full-page, eight-column *Toledo Blade* article that described the Lasalle & Koch Company's achievement proclaimed the opening as much more than a mere expansion of shopping possibilities for Toledoans and the store itself as one of the monuments of the city:

A photo of the store along Huron Street shows the lively and inviting composition of elements that characterized the building. *By permission of the Toledo-Lucas County Library.*

It is customary to say that a new and sturdy building is a monument to the genius and enterprise of its builders, a present memorial to the vision of the men who could see far enough ahead to know that their community was big enough in spirit and going to be big enough in body to appreciate and to patronize. The Lasalle & Koch store is all of that, and it is more. It is a monument to the city of Toledo. It singles out this city as enterprising enough and "metropolitan" enough to deserve and to vindicate the finest store in America. It is not too much to say that with the opening of this store Toledo enters upon a new mercantile era—an era of bigger and finer things than she has ever dreamed of.

It was true that the store immediately became a monument. In its proportions, it was to Toledo and to the retail world in general what the building of the *Titanic* five years earlier was to transportation. Only it didn't sink; it went from success to success. The retail map of Toledo was forever changed; it was the older and lesser stores that stayed on Summit Street, while they could. The "new retail order" made Adams Street the "main draw" of Toledo, with the Lion Store and smaller retailers serving as an eastern anchor and the whole presided over at its west end by Lasalle's. The later location of the Lamson Brothers Company on Huron Street and Toledo's late and deeply lamented Paramount Theater right across Adams Street from Lasalle's are proof positive of the great store's effect on the city's core.

To what degree this development caught the eye of one of America's largest retail organizations cannot be easily ascertained, but five years after the opening of the Lasalle & Koch store on Adams, a small announcement in the *New York Times* is a good indicator that it did.

The Larger Lasalle & Koch Store

Eventually, the euphoria surrounding the opening of the new Lasalle & Koch store diminished, and the store simply took its place as a major downtown anchor, and the largest of the Three *L*s. The corner of Adams and Huron soon came to be known as the "Hub of Toledo," and the store others called too ambitious, too impractical and too far north of Summit Street to meet with success was doing in one month the amount of business transacted in one year at its older home on Jefferson Street.

One organization that paid attention to the success Alfred B. Koch wrought in Toledo was R.H. Macy & Company of New York. Of course, the name Macy's hardly needs introduction or elaboration. It is useful, though, to uncover a bit of Macy's history in order to better comprehend how Lasalle's came to be one of its subsidiaries.

R.H. Macy & Company was founded in 1858 on Sixth Street in New York City, when Rowland H. Macy began a dry goods concern at thirty-six years of age. Reared on Nantucket, Massachusetts, the rough-and-tumble Macy, who eventually had a red star tattooed on his hand, lived a checkered life marred by adventuresome schemes and business failures. After spending the last four years of his teens serving on a whaling ship in the Pacific Ocean, he returned to Massachusetts to work at various positions in Boston dry goods stores of the day. Lack of success prompted him to take off for California, which was in the throes of the gold rush. The store he opened in Marysville, California, failed within months, causing Macy to return east and settle in the small town of Haverhill, Massachusetts, where he again tried his hand at dry goods retailing and again met with failure after four years of hard work beset with misfortune.

After a stint as a stockbroker in Boston and a spell in Superior, Wisconsin, Macy made the realization that his repeated failures as a shopkeeper were due to the fact that he was applying big-city retail methods in small-town markets. His next stop was New York City, where his newest venture was a tremendous success, eventually gobbling up adjacent properties and growing into a full-line department store by 1870. Yet Macy only produced one heir, Rowland Jr., who apparently did not inherit any of his father's good qualities and died in tragic circumstances in 1878, one year after his father passed away on a buying trip to Paris.

Two of Macy's managing partners (one of whom was his nephew) bought out Macy's estate and continued the business. A string of unfortunate circumstances, which read like a Victorian soap opera, saw one partner succumb to disease and a third pass away, leaving a widow who then married the company's fourth partner, who brought his nephew on to manage the store until the partner was bought out in a battle between partners in 1887. In spite of the internal drama, the store continued to expand and was modernized behind a uniform façade. Even an early example of a department store tearoom was opened at the popular and growing store.

During this period, when the remains of Macy's management was exhausted, to say the least, the store's crockery department was leased to Lazarus Straus & Sons. When the remaining partner, Charles B. Webster, was ready to exit the retail business, brothers Isidor and Nathan Straus bought the whole organization. Under Straus control, R.H. Macy & Company went from strength to strength, moving in 1902 to an elegant new building with ornate Palladian details on Herald Square, where it remains today, one of few American department stores to have done its business in only two locations for a history spanning over one hundred years. The Straus dynasty lasted for five generations at Macy's, despite Isidor's untimely death on the *Titanic* in April 1912.

Macy's added a floor to its beautiful premises on Herald Square in 1910 and expanded westward from its Broadway storefront toward Seventh Avenue with the addition of a twenty-story tower in 1924. When art deco additions were added in 1928 and 1931, the building stretched all the way to Seventh Avenue and could proclaim itself the "World's Largest Store," with over 2.3 million square feet of space spread throughout its buildings.

Yet size alone has never been the only thing that has made Macy's a nationally renowned retail name. Under its slogan "It's Smart to be Thrifty," it offered New Yorkers the widest possible selection of high-quality goods at the best prices, from designer apparel in its famous Little Shop to antiques in its Corner Shop on the eighth floor. It sold a huge array of groceries and gourmet items in its Fancy Grocery and became a part of wider American culture through its Thanksgiving Day Parade, broadcast from coast to coast; its role in the popular Christmas film *Miracle on Thirty-fourth Street*; and a great variety of other events and promotions. Its annual flower show transformed the store into a botanical showcase of breathtaking beauty, and at the same time, the store had the ability to turn something as simple as an after-hours guard dog bearing a litter into a celebrated window display that attracted huge crowds, not to mention the business associated with them.

Macy's had an in-house bureau of standards, which assured that its merchandise was worthy, and a staff "taster," who had the last word on any foodstuffs sold in the store. Its advertising department coined the phrase "Does Macy's Tell Gimbels?" to promote Macy's comparison-shopping bureau, which worked to make sure it could honestly say that the store was never undersold.

By the time that the Lasalle & Koch Company built its flagship in Toledo, Macy's profit was so great that it went shopping for other retailers in order to create a nationwide department store chain that could take its reputation to other markets. At about this time, the profits from Lasalle's increase in business at the new location allowed Alfred B. Koch to purchase 100 percent of the store's remaining stock in the hands of the Lasalle & Koch families. He did so not to wrest sole control of the store but to seek a partner who could help it expand and grow, which, according to contemporary reports, Koch felt "to be in keeping with the progressive merchandising tendencies of the times."

Accordingly, R.H. Macy & Company purchased what it called "an interest" in the Lasalle & Koch Company. The deal caused such a stir in New York and Toledo when it was announced that Macy's prompted the *New York Times* to print a correction that clearly stated that the giant retailer purchased only "an interest" in the Lasalle & Koch Company and that "control" remained with Alfred B. Koch, who would select the Toledo store's board of directors and himself sit on Macy's board as well.

Decidedly unlike the 2006 changeover of many local department store names to the Federated Department Store Macy's brand, the early twentieth-century Macy's valued the local orientation of Lasalle & Koch's and vowed to keep the name and business practices the same as they had been. Over time, though, Lasalle's took on some aspects of a "Junior Macy's" that were hard to deny. By the 1950s, the graphic designs of Lasalle's advertisements were similar to those of Macy's in New York; the store featured famous Macy house brands, such as "Supre-Macy"; and Lasalle's had developed its own version of the Little Shop for designer apparel. Yet the store also went out of its way to identify with Toledo and downplay its New York associations for the most part.

A fascinating sidelight to the Lasalle's and Macy's merger is that the large New York concern went on a buying spree afterward that did take it from coast to coast by 1949. In 1925, Macy's acquired the Davison-Paxon Company of Atlanta, where it built a new flagship store. Architects for the building were none other than Starrett and van Vleck, who designed a massive brick structure with a high main floor, a bowed elevator bank and modern-leaning Georgian stone detail that bears a stripped-down resemblance to their work in Toledo.

L. Bamberger & Company of Newark was bought next, in 1929, and after World War II, the O'Connor Moffat Company of San Francisco and the William Taylor Dry Goods Company of Kansas City became part of the Macy organization. These latter two were the only stores whose names changed to Macy's as the big New York concern grew. In spite of its size, Macy's let each of its divisions operate locally, and while they were clearly subsidiaries of the great New York store, each developed its own character and identity. Macy's of California was always more chic and fashionable than its New York parent, and Davison's retained an air of Southern charm. Bamberger's own character was firmly rooted in its New Jersey home.

In most cases, these stores went on to become regional powerhouses by acquisition of smaller retailers in the area. Macy's of Kansas City spread to Wichita, Kansas, and Joplin, Missouri, by acquiring the George Innes Company and the Christman Dry Goods Company, respectively. In other cases, the stores built branches in smaller towns in the vicinity. For the most part, each of these divisions eventually took on a regional character while operating from a local headquarters. Lasalle's was among them.

On February 1, 1927, Alfred B. Koch surprised Toledo by making the announcement that Lasalle's would expand its premises, which was less than ten years old. The company would spend a quarter of a million dollars to add three floors to the structure, which would be remodeled and reconfigured as a result. Citing the industrial growth of Toledo, Koch said that "the Lasalle & Koch Company will do its part to join Toledo in its metropolitan trend" and that "this enlargement of the store is merely an expression of our great faith in the future of Toledo and an effort on our part to make shopping easy for customers."

The LASALLE & KOCH Co.

Before-and-after comparison of the Lasalle & Koch store as originally built and as expanded in 1927. *From an ad, collection of the author.*

A fall opening date was predicted for the "Larger Lasalle & Koch Store," and preliminary sketches showed a new ninth floor and two floors of recessed penthouses composing the tenth and eleventh floors. The addition would add seventy-five thousand square feet to the structure, and A. Bentley & Sons, the Toledo contractor who built Lasalle's ten years earlier, was hired to construct the additions.

To celebrate the upcoming opening of its enlarged store, Lasalle & Koch's planned an exhibition of paintings by noted muralist Arthur Covey. Covey, born in Illinois, gained fame as an artist by depicting workers in industry. One of his best-known works—murals for the Kohler Company of Wisconsin that featured images of the company's workers in its factories—were conceived to "ennoble their work in the minds of the workers themselves," according to the *Blade*'s article about the Toledo artwork. Covey's wife, Lois Lenski, was an author and illustrator who gained fame for her popular children's books.

The store announced the upcoming opening, ten years to the day after moving to Adams and Huron, through a series of ads recalling Toledo's recent history and progress. The notices also referred to the Lasalle & Koch Company's "Ten Golden Years" in its new home. Beginning on November 2, 1927, the store's show windows were given over to Covey's work, and an

The Lasalle & Koch Co.

Artist's rendering of how the "Larger Lasalle & Koch Store" would look after the addition of three floors. *By permission of the Toledo-Lucas County Library.*

evening unveiling ceremony, which culminated in the simultaneous raising of the windows' curtains to reveal the artwork, was jammed with people crowding the sidewalks in order to catch a glimpse of the murals.

Seventeen of the unique black-and-white canvasses, painted on a silver background, portrayed the progress of Toledo's indigenous industries, Libbey Glass, the Willys-Overland Company and Toledo Scale among them. Two other paintings showed the "Toledo of Yesterday" and "Toledo of Today." For twelve days, not a piece of merchandise was shown in Lasalle's windows so that the public could enjoy the art exhibition.

The larger Lasalle & Koch Store opened for inspection on Saturday evening, November 12, 1927. The following Monday, the store was open for business in the throes of a ten-day-long "Achievement Sale," which offered special prices on merchandise to celebrate what the company had accomplished since moving to the corner of Adams and Huron. Lasalle's newly redesigned restaurants on the eighth floor didn't reopen until the fifteenth, according to an announcement in the paper, which invited customers to make a reservation. "Several months ago, Toledo's favorite luncheon rendezvous went into temporary retirement, and many a palate has languished since. At that time we promised adequate compensation for the enforced cessation of hospitalities, and tomorrow you may judge if we have kept our promise. A suggestion of the decoration of the French Room is illustrated here. Other rooms are the English Room and the Early American Room. Everybody will want to be present at the opening!"

The main benefit to customers in the enlarged store was a new ninth floor completely given over to the display and sale of furniture. The removal of merchandise to this new floor caused a general rearrangement of the store, and the new tenth and eleventh floors housed service facilities whose previous space could be used for the benefit of merchandising.

Completely new facilities for employees occupied the eleventh floor, including a hospital, lounge rooms and an employee cafeteria. The tenth floor was occupied by a large receiving room, as well as offices and workspace for Lasalle & Koch's advertising and display staff. As mentioned above, a complete reconfiguration of the eighth-floor restaurants and auditorium took up that floor, prompting the *Toledo Blade* to remark that "the masterpiece of artistry is the main dining room or 'French' room. The color combinations and blending of the walls, the carpeting, the chairs and tables themselves and the indirect lighting effects produce an amazing effect, the first glimpse of which brings a gasp of astonishment and admiration. Three other dining rooms known as the Early American room, the English room, and the Grill Room are also beautifully furnished."

Other features of the store, such as a reconfigured main floor, new elevators and the first installation of the "Symphony Tone"—a public address, music and paging system—were duly noted in the press, and the enormous "Achievement Sale" was touted as "a day of golden savings for every year of golden growth at Adams and Huron Streets."

To sum up what the Lasalle & Koch Company's accomplishments represented for Toledo, the *Blade* wrote:

> *These things which have been done in the enlargement and beautification of this palace of merchandising have been done because the vision and wisdom of the management indicated that they were justified by the advancement of Toledo. Faith in this community and its citizens and the desire to give adequate*

Dramatic corner shot of the expanded store. Of the three floors added, only the ninth is visible from the street. *By permission of the Toledo-Lucas County Library.*

service to their ever-developing demands actuated the management in its present program far more than any other factor. Executives long have been convinced that the city has proved itself "metropolitan" enough and the citizenship has proved themselves to be enterprising enough to deserve this greatest store in America.

Though the Great Depression lay ahead, not to mention World War II, Lasalle's "achievement," as indicated by the above quote, was not just for and about the store. Directly across Adams Street, on February 16, 1929, the Publix Theatre Company opened Toledo's glorious Paramount Theatre to the public. On the next block westward, in the 1930s, fashion retailer Stein's located a new five-story store sheathed in a Moderne-style stone-clad exterior, again right on the Adams and Huron corner. Lasalle's achievement had an infectious quality that grew beyond the retailer itself.

The Lasalle & Koch Company weathered the Depression under Alfred B. Koch's leadership, and the store was witness to several events of note during the 1930s. For many years, a nearly four-foot-tall rooster weathervane sat atop one of the store's water tanks and became something of a Toledo landmark as well as a store mascot. The history of the weathervane is an amusing one. A political discussion between Alfred B. Koch, a dedicated Republican, and Jacob Lehnertz, a leading Democrat and manager of the popular Dyer's Chop House restaurant, ended in a bet. If Herbert Hoover won the 1932 presidential election, Lehnertz would have to pay for a weathervane sporting an elephant symbol atop the Lasalle & Koch store; conversely, if Franklin D. Roosevelt won, Koch would pay to erect a weathervane with a rooster (a symbol of the Democrat Party at the time) atop his store. Alfred B. Koch lost the bet and was compelled to pay for the eighteen-foot-tall weathervane, whose rooster itself stood forty-two inches high. The weathervane sat atop the store for the next thirty-six years and was often illustrated, along with the three iconic water tanks, in Lasalle's promotional advertising.

Also in the 1930s, Lasalle's hosted a "Foreign Fair," for which the store's auditorium was turned into a street of shops offering imported goods. Neiman-Marcus of Dallas is generally credited with inventing the department store "import fair" in the fall of 1957, when it hosted its first "Fortnight," which brought French merchandise and culture to the Texas store over a two-week period. Though the Lasalle's event predated Neiman's "Fortnights" by many years, the practice was widely imitated by many department stores in the 1960s and early 1970s as a way of generating traffic. Lasalle's repeated the practice in the 1960s as well.

The city of Toledo celebrated its hundredth anniversary in 1936, and Lasalle's celebrated its seventy-second anniversary together with it. The store issued public service advertisements that showed the parallel growth of Lasalle's along with the city. On the hundredth anniversary of the date of the consolidation of Port Lawrence and Vistula, the Lasalle & Koch Company

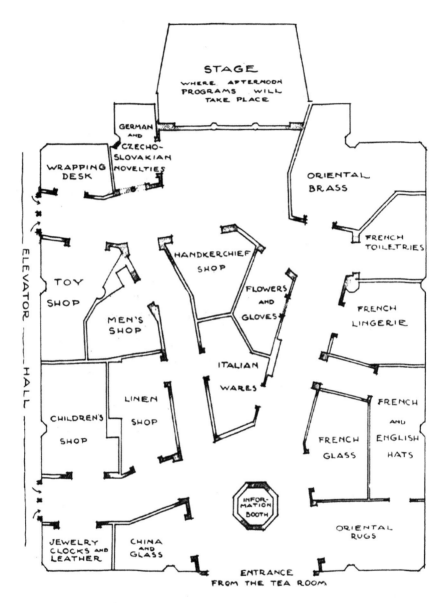

This map will help you to see everything.

Lasalle's "Foreign Fair" held in the eighth-floor auditorium in the 1930s. Lasalle's hired architects Gerow, Conklin & Hobbs to design the exhibit, and assistance was provided by the International Institute of Toledo and the Toledo Art Museum School of Design. *From the Business & Industry of Greater Toledo Collection, Toledo-Lucas County Public Library.*

mounted a plaque commemorating the event on the outside of its store at the precise location where the dividing line between the two townships passed under the store. In its advertising, Lasalle's noted that "Toledo sprang from the union of two rival pioneer towns a hundred years ago, and Lasalle & Koch's springs tall and proud from the earth of both."

Alfred B. Koch died suddenly of a heart attack while watching a wrestling match in November 1937. Eulogies in the day's papers summed up Koch's work not only as a promoter of his own business but also as a member of the board of the Toledo Art Museum and a volunteer with the Boy Scouts, the Red Cross and the Toledo Community Chest, among other organizations. The tragedy of his unexpected and early death at the age of fifty-three was muted somewhat by the words of the *Toledo News-Bee*, which stated that "under Alfred Koch, the Lasalle & Koch store became a civic institution, and Alfred Koch became a civic figure. He and the store were inseparably united in the minds of the people of Toledo." Alfred B. Koch was buried in Collingwood Memorial after a brief service conducted by the pastor of Collingwood Avenue Presbyterian Church.

Alas, individual memories are the only present way to get a personal insight into the nature of shopping in a store such as Lasalle's. Sarah Hogoboom, from as far away as Wisconsin, experienced Lasalle's on summer visits to the Glass City:

> *We spent every summer in Toledo with mother's family. My aunt Jean and her husband, Dr. Ben Gilette, had no children, so Aunt Jean doted on my sister and me. She outfitted us in lovely clothes from Toledo's best stores. On a typical shopping trip to Lasalle & Koch's, Aunt Jean would settle herself on a banquette in the juvenile department and the sales clerk would bring out dresses for her approval. Then, my sister and I would model them for her before making choices. The summer I started college in Madison, Aunt Jean took me shopping at Lasalle's for a winter coat. My sister got one too. She had the coats shipped to us in Wisconsin in order to avoid Ohio sales tax. One of the department stores, probably Lasalle's, sponsored a style show at the Toledo Yacht Club, and my sister and I got to be models. Of course, my mother and Aunt Jean and all the Toledo family are gone now. But I can close my eyes and picture these lovely stores and the beautiful things we bought on our shopping trips. It's a wonderful chance to reminisce!*

The late first lady Betty Ford grew up in Grand Rapids, Michigan, and worked at Herpolsheimer's, one of the city's foremost department stores.

When she married in 1942, she settled with her husband, William Warren, in Maumee. She took a job at Lasalle & Koch's as a "demonstrator" who modeled clothes at lunchtime in the eighth-floor dining rooms in addition to completing selling and office work at other times of the day. In spite of the failure of her first marriage, she made quite an impression during lunch at Lasalle's as a "stunning" model before she met future president Gerald Ford.

Lasalle & Koch's continued into the 1940s under the leadership of Louis Eppstein, Alfred B. Koch's friend and colleague. Eppstein himself accepted the presidency of the store, saying, "I could have anticipated no greater honor in my life than to succeed the position held so nobly by my lifelong friend and business associate, Alfred Koch." Soon after, he reassured employees of Lasalle's by saying that "Alfred Koch was a great organizer. The staff of this store is okay; it suits me. There will be no changes."

Changes come inevitably, and the entry of the United States into World War II in 1941 saw many of those employees give service to their country. Eppstein himself retired in 1940 (though he remained on the board of directors until his death in 1945) and was replaced by Richard Lennihan, a Macy's executive from New York. When the United States and its allies emerged victoriously from World War II, Lasalle's was not only still in business but also ready to grow in the postwar era.

Branches in the Great Black Swamp

It has already been established that the postwar branch development program of R.H. Macy & Company and its subsidiaries focused on building a regional presence for its stores. Lasalle's was a typical case in point. With its large and popular store in Downtown Toledo, it postponed suburban shopping center developments until new branches could be developed in the smaller cities of northwestern Ohio.

The war wasn't even over in December 1944 when the Lasalle & Koch Company announced that it had purchased the fifty-five-year-old business of A. Froney & Company, a department store located on South Main Street in Bowling Green, Ohio. In speaking about the store, president Lennihan assured citizens of the town that, while the name of the Froney establishment would change on January 15 of the next year, the store would continue its policies that made Froney's "a synonym for quality, fair dealing, courtesy and real friendliness." In addition, he vowed that as soon as the war was over and materials were again available, the store would install a new storefront and remodel its facilities, making it "physically the outstanding small city store in Ohio."

Opposite: Streamlined 1930s illustration of Lasalle & Koch's, one of few to show the building's landmark water towers and rooster weathervane. *From an ad, collection of the author.*

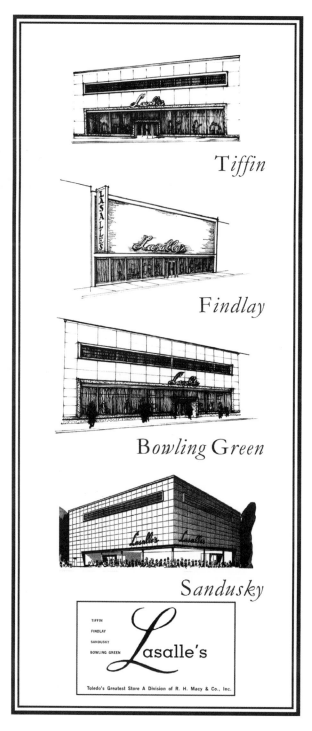

Tiffin

Findlay

Bowling Green

Sandusky

Lasalle's early branches were located in the downtown districts of northwestern Ohio cities, giving the retailer a regional presence. *Collection of the author.*

Eventually, a sleek, modern front was installed at 139 South Main Street, and Lasalle's became an anchor in the downtown area. Not long afterward, a new store in Tiffin, Ohio, was announced. With a façade similar to the Bowling Green store, the new building opened on August 21, 1947, at 71 South Washington Street in the town's core. The grand opening was characterized by the cutting of a white ribbon and accompanied by a brass band. Over three thousand eager shoppers toured the 29,000-square-foot facility on its opening day.

At the same time, Lasalle's purchased property in Findlay for a similar store but, two months after the gala opening of the Tiffin branch, revealed plans for a larger store in downtown Sandusky, east of Toledo. On October 29, 1947, the *Sandusky Register-Star News* informed the public that Lasalle & Koch's had purchased the old Sloane Block at Columbus Avenue and Washington Row and intended to raze it to construct the largest of its outlying branches.

Two years later, the three-story branch, clad in Indiana limestone and Cold Spring granite, opened to the public. The *Register-Star News* described the layout of the store in detail, noting its "restful colors" and special features, such as a full-service beauty salon and basement luncheonette. A daylong grand opening celebration was attended by Macy's officials from New York and featured performances by the Sandusky High School band. Ladies attending the opening were each presented with an orchid, flown in from Hawaii for the event.

As mentioned, Lasalle's bought property for a fourth outlying store, in Findlay, Ohio, in 1946, but the project was postponed until an announcement was made in November 1954 that management finally gave the "go-ahead" for a 34,000-square-foot store at 514 South Main Street in the city forty-six miles south of Toledo. Like its predecessors, the store was jammed with customers on its opening day, August 15, 1955, and it featured a similarly modern front that, at the time, was said to "harmonize well with the improvements shopkeepers are making on Main Street."

Though she now lives in Michigan, retired educator Nancy Pihlaja, née Barlage, grew up on a farm in the small town of Miller City, west of Findlay, Ohio. Her memories are an indicator of what Lasalle's early branch stores meant to people of the area, characterized by neat, well-kept towns more often than not populated by descendants of early German settlers. "My mother would go into Findlay twice a year to shop," she recalled, "and while we weren't typical Lasalle's customers, if she was looking for something really special, of course that's where we went. I remember being intrigued by the elevator that had a person to operate it and tell you what was on each floor. We went up to the second floor—and that was a big deal in those days, especially for a girl from such a small town. Later, when I was older and could go to Findlay on my own, I liked to walk around Lasalle's and browse the merchandise because it was all so beautiful and well presented."

With this fourth store, Lasalle's became the dominant department store not just of Toledo but also the whole northwestern Ohio area once known as the "Great Black Swamp." The company during this time did not neglect its flagship store in Toledo, nor did Macy's cease to supply its Toledo subsidiary with managerial talent groomed at its New York base.

Customers saw postwar progress at Lasalle's just a few years after peace returned. In 1947, the store installed its first escalators and carried out remodeling on the main floor. Each of these projects still had to be approved by the Civilian Production Board before construction could begin. The more modern atmosphere created during this time eliminated some of the grandeur of Lasalle's main floor by covering the stone walls in a more prosaic plaster finish in order to hide duct shafts which were added for air-conditioning. Another, more thorough remodeling was undertaken in 1956.

The great height of the main floor complicated escalator installation, because it would be impossible to install an escalator that could make the run to the second floor without a break. A landing mezzanine was built to accommodate the new conveyance, though it also diminished the "admirable vistas and magnificent distances" so admired in earlier years. By the midcentury, however, convenience, rather than classical beauty and proportion, was at the forefront of customers' minds, and Lasalle's had to keep up with the times. Tiedtke's and Sears were the only other stores in Toledo with escalators; the Lion Store didn't get them until 1962, and Lamson's relied on elevators in its flagship store for the rest of its existence.

Jamie Farr specifically recalled the store's "magnificent, beautiful Christmas decorations" as a reason to come downtown shopping in the postwar era, but in reality, there were many. Lasalle's observed an anniversary sale each September, as well as white sales, housewares festivals, Toledo Day sales and many other regular events. It was a quirk of fate that saw each of the Three *L*s founded in September, and all three were able to compete with anniversary sale events around the same time of the year.

Lasalle's managerial leadership at the time was usually culled from the Macy's headquarters in New York. However, the store's able executives, no matter where they came from, carried on Lasalle's traditions of community involvement and made sure that Toledoans conceived of the store as an important local business worthy of their patronage. By the time Richard

Lennihan retired in 1949, Macy's had already sent future president Michael Yamin to Toledo in order to be ready to take the reins of the store when necessary. A Macy's employee since 1924, Yamin was vice-president of Bamberger's in New Jersey at the time of his transfer to Toledo as vice-president of the Lasalle & Koch Company, serving as general supervisor of operations under the soon-to-retire Lennihan.

It was under Michael Yamin's leadership that the store pursued branch development in the Toledo area, undertook many special events and, perhaps most challengingly, guided the store through a dark period in 1957, when ten unions representing employees of Lamson's, Lasalle's and the Lion Store walked out of contract negotiations with Retail Associates, Inc., the bargaining committee for the three stores. Tiedtke's settled one day after the strike began and left Retail Associates, avoiding further problems at its store.

Pickets were set up at Lasalle's in November, just prior to the all-important Christmas selling season. The situation rapidly deteriorated as the stores sought to have limits placed on the picketing at Lasalle's entrances, and the courts, and later the National Labor Relations Board, became involved. The situation reached its nadir in January 1958. Nine of the ten unions representing retail employees ratified a contract with the stores, but the Retail Clerks International Association, the largest of these bodies, voted to continue the strike. Subsequently, Lasalle's downtown store and two of its branches were attacked with "stench bombs"; a few days later, an unidentified person released thirty-five mice and three pigeons at the main store, causing pandemonium among customers and employees. Picketing spread to Lamson's, too, and it wasn't until after much legal action on a local and national level that a volunteer "Labor-Management-Citizens Committee" was able to negotiate an end to the strike in December 1958.

In spite of an earlier failure to accomplish the same objective, the committee, led by Monsignor Michael J. Doyle, was able to convince both parties to end the strike. Monsignor Doyle took action as an individual to negotiate between the parties before taking on the chairmanship of the LMC Committee, promoting an equitable settlement for both sides. With resolution coming on Christmas Eve, the clergyman noted:

It is not without significance that after negotiations had seemingly become hopelessly deadlocked and the strike had every appearance of being protracted for months and perhaps even years, a settlement was effected on the eve of the great feast that marks the birth of the Prince of Peace, when Heaven, through angelic choristers, sent to earth a most meaningful message: "Peace...to men of good will'....In the kindly, friendly, conciliatory approach that has characterized the negotiations in the past few weeks, former strikers should return to their jobs with nothing but good will in their hearts and, in the same spirit of good will, should be received and welcomed by management and their fellow employees. Even the slightest gesture of recrimination would violate the good will that is so essential a condition to the climate of mutual trust, future harmonious relationships, and the peace of heart that is born only of good will.

It must be assumed that the shared spirit of good will did take place between Lasalle's and its employees, for the store carried on with its plans and continued to serve the public as the dominant department store of northwestern Ohio. The conflict continued in the courts, though, until 1969, when the Sixth Circuit Court of Appeals in Cincinnati settled an ongoing disagreement between Lasalle's and the Retail Store Employees Union by judging that the LMC Committee's ability to stay involved and negotiate grievances ended with the contract which expired in 1960.

During the strike, though, Lasalle's presented one of the most spectacular special events for which it had developed a reputation. Macy's in New York City had for many years presented an elaborate flower show on the main floor of its enormous flagship store. Taking a cue from this tradition, Lasalle's undertook months of planning to present an equivalent show to Toledo. President Yamin and the store's display division worked with local florists and national and global suppliers of plant material to provide live and cut floral materials for display on the main floor and in each of the street-side display windows. The displays were designed to imitate gardens and flower markets of differing countries and U.S. states that were noted for the beauty of their indigenous flora.

The flower show's presentation was staggering, involving special refrigeration necessary to keep plants fresh and healthy for the six-day show. Live birch trees were trucked in from New Jersey, and greenhouses across the country forced blooms on some plants and retarded others with cold temperatures in order to coordinate arrival of perfect plant material for the May 19 opening date. During the duration of the show, forty thousand cut flowers were completely changed three times, and a nightly brigade of gardeners hydrated the plants and freshened anything that needed attention. Of its show, which caused a sensation in Toledo, Lasalle's informed the public:

You'll walk right into a garden wonderland when you visit Lasalle's Flower Show...our bouquet to Toledo. Step into Lasalle's, and you'll know how Alice felt when she stepped through the Looking Glass! Over 30,000 square feet of our Main Floor has been transformed into a breath-taking botanical garden—a spectacle as lavish as the Hanging Gardens of Babylon. Thrill to bank after bank of flowering shrubs and foliage... groves of full-grown budding birch trees towering over two-stories high... exotic plants from Hawaii, the South Pacific, California...thousands of sweet-smelling blossoms. You'll be fascinated by our windows...[where you'll] *see "flowers of the nations" in living bloom! You'll be dazzled, delighted, enchanted—by the color, the fragrance, the beauty, and the sheer size of Lasalle's news-making Flower Show...the most beautiful bouquet we could gather for you!*

In 1961, Lasalle's announced that it would finally build a branch store in Toledo, revealing that the A.S. Bentley & Sons Company, which had built its home so many years ago, would construct a sleek new store in Westgate Village. The store was designed by noted West Coast architect John Savage Bolles, who was responsible for, among other things, Caesar's Palace in Las Vegas. His work for Macy's of California was characterized by delicate concrete detailing that endowed the potentially monotonous large buildings with an interesting sense of depth due to the play of light that resulted from his creativity.

The 152,000-square-foot store eventually opened on February 19, 1962, and its perforated, overhanging second floor indeed carried on architect Bolles's fascination with the light-and-shadow play of openings in concrete, even though the effect would of necessity be mitigated due to Toledo's climate naturally being less sunny overall than California's.

Another unique aspect of the store at the time of its opening was the installation of *Lumia*, the work of Danish-born artist Thomas Wilfred. *Lumia*, which consisted of a keyboard that drove projected images of color on a darkened surface, was described by the artist as "a concert of light without sound" and had been shown to the royal courts of Denmark and Great Britain. The installation was even used to accompany a concert of the Philadelphia Orchestra, in which the great Leopold Stokowski conducted a performance of Nikolai Rimsky-Koraskov's symphonic suite *Sheherezade*.

Lumia was projected nightly during the grand opening on a fifty-three- by twenty-six-foot recessed surface over the store's main entrance. Louise Bruner, art editor for the *Blade* at the time, cautioned that viewers who anticipated a large-scale kaleidoscope or an abstract painting projected on a wall would find *Lumia* to be neither. Her account is perhaps the best description of a piece of art that was, for the most part, impossible to preserve:

Lasalle's Westgate store was a sleek midmodern design that was eventually joined by an auto center on the shopping center property. *Collection of the author.*

This is an art form geared to the space age, where man, himself is traveling at a fantastic rate of speed on his own planet. It speaks in new dimensions, like photographs of the surface of our world taken by a camera in an orbiting satellite. It also absorbs the uncharted realms of the imagination, producing the kind of pictures we see in glowing embers, in cloud formations at sunset, and in our dreams. Flying objects flash by and burst into a golden shower. Slithering phantom fish glide past a silvery sea, disappearing into a yawning purple cavern that expands into a field of azure and topaz flowers. A flow of cherry-red lava rushes forward to engulf prehistoric monsters, gyrating in a frenzied dance. Wispy pink smoke flames into intense orange, trailing threads of glittering glass…The main objective is that the pictures are as fleeting as a smile.

Another event planned for the opening of the Westgate Lasalle's was an exhibit of children's artwork from the Toledo Museum of Art. Apparently no descriptions survive that could determine whether those works evoked as much discussion as *Lumia* did. Wilfred's opus, however, has been universally admired and has been exhibited as far away as the Centre Pompidou in Paris. Though small recreations of *Lumia* can be seen online, how the installation appeared on the face of a midcentury modern department store in Toledo must rely, sadly, only on the imagination.

The store itself was Lasalle's first big, full-line branch store in the manner that was becoming increasingly popular around the country. On its two levels, it featured not just sales areas but also amenities such as a community auditorium (first used for the above-mentioned juvenile art exhibition) and a popular restaurant called the "Terrace Room," which had a second-floor view over the Westgate Village complex. Newspaper reports praised the variety of color used in the interior design, from "soft mauves and purples in the Little Shop to gay orange, mustards and beiges in the children's area at the other end of the building." The store's major fixtures were composed of grained walnut with brushed antique gold accents, and the "sophisticated" murals that added artistry to the interior were executed by nationally known artists William Riggs and Howard Pederson.

Abbot Justin DuVall remembers that his mother, Nancy, was to be transferred from her job downtown when the new Westgate store opened:

She actually resented it, because she was used to the downtown store, and was determined to stay there, until she realized that it was just the newness of it all that frightened her. So she said, "You know what? I'm going to put in for a transfer!" She became the first woman in the furniture department at Lasalle's, and was teased, but in a friendly way, by the salesmen at Westgate. It's amazing to think that because of her training as an apparel saleswoman, she always took care over our clothing purchases; we could never buy anything that didn't match the quality she learned to appreciate at Lasalle's. But she didn't know a thing about furniture. I can still see her pouring over Lasalle's ads in order to learn the merchandise, and she became an excellent salesperson, as knowledgeable about furniture as she had been about clothing. Eventually, she became a member of the store's Twenty-Five-Year Club and earned an $89.95-a-month pension, which she always referred to as her "Little Pension." Of course, social security kicked in, and she was able to retire fairly comfortably and even went back to work at the store on a temporary basis to cover vacations and sales events at Westgate and, occasionally, downtown.

Nancy related a few other amusing stories about her experiences at Lasalle's to her son. She often spoke about the diplomacy required in dealing with customers when the store's image was at stake. She was trained to quietly tell customers with overdrawn credit cards, "Can you wait a moment while I check on something," before she went to get a manager to deal with the situation. By the time Nancy worked at Westgate, the future Benedictine

*L*asalle's <u>Westgate</u> *is simply the m*

COME BE DAZZLED, TODAY...WHEN WE OPEN

INTO A BRIGHT, GLAMOROUS   WORI

FRESH ASSORTMENTS OF EVERYTHING FROM THE |

DISCOVER PRACTICALLY EVERY DEPARTMENT YOU

STILL CARRIES LASALLE'S FAMOUS HONEST PRICI

TERRACE ROOM   RESTAURANT AND LUXL

ART FROM THE TOLEDO MUSEUM CLASSES. AND

THE 'LUMIA'   ART OF LIGHT CONC

BEAUTIFUL LASALLE'S WESTGATE, A STORE YOU

Now you can have *L*asalle's any way yo

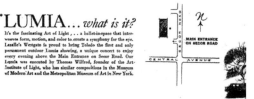

'LUMIA... *what is it?*

It's the fascinating Art of Light , . . . a ballet-in-space that inter-
weaves form, motion, and color to create a symphony for the eye.
Lasalle's Westgate is proud to bring Toledo the first and only
permanent outdoor Lumia showing, a unique concert to enjoy
every evening above the Main Entrance on Secor Road. Our
Lumia was executed by Thomas Wilfred, founder of the Art-
Institute of Light, who has similar compositions in the Museum
of Modern Art and the Metropolitan Museum of Art in New York.

LASALLE'S DOWNTOWN OPEN LATE MONDAY AND

A lavish, two-page spread in the newspapers outlined the grand-opening events planned for Lasalle's first suburban Toledo store. *Collection of the author.*

ost beautiful store you've ever seen

THE DOORS AT 11 A.M. STEP FROM OUR 1000-CAR FREE PARKING LOT

LD OF SHOPPING JOY. STROLL THROUGH SPACIOUS AISLES; DELIGHT IN SPARKLING

NEWEST FASHIONS TO MARVELOUS HOME FURNISHINGS

LOVE IN LASALLE'S DOWNTOWN. NOTE THAT ALL THIS BEAUTY AND CONVENIENCE

E TAGS. OBSERVE HOW WE PAMPER YOU WITH PLEASURES LIKE A BREATHTAKING

JRIOUS ANTOINE BEAUTY SALON. ENJOY OUR AUDITORIUM EXHIBIT OF CHILDREN'S

DON'T MISS THE AFTER-DARK SPECTACULAR THAT WILL THRILL ALL TOLEDO...

:ERT OVER THE MAIN ENTRANCE. THIS AND MUCH MORE IS WAITING FOR YOU AT

SIMPLY WON'T WANT TO LEAVE EVEN THOUGH IT'S OPEN EVERY NIGHT 'TIL 9:30.

u like us... Downtown or Suburban Style

THURSDAY 'TIL 9 P.M. LASALLE'S WESTGATE OPEN EVERY DAY 9:30 A.M. 'TIL 9:30 P.M.

"Italia Magnifica" was the first of Lasalle's three import fairs held in the 1960s. *Collection of the author.*

abbot visited his mom on his own. On one occasion, she pointed out what she considered to be a flaw in the design of the store. Exit stairs from the second floor let out directly to the building's first floor vestibules. She recalled how thieves on several occasions walked furniture right off the sales floor and down the stairs. If an employee noticed and sounded an emergency alarm, the culprits simply dropped the furniture down the stairs and made a hasty escape through the vestibule.

At the time, like many department stores, Lasalle's began to differentiate itself from other retailers by using the store-within-a-store concept, which separated merchandise areas into smaller, themed boutiques in order to make the shopping experience (in a gigantic store) more of an intimate one. Lasalle's boutiques—such as the Little Shop, Country Corner (casual sports apparel for women), Beach Shop, Mustang Shop (for young men's apparel), Young World (Children's wear) and the Colonial Shop (period furniture)—were replicated, albeit in smaller versions, in Westgate as well.

Two years later, in 1964, Lasalle's once again staged an event that had been pioneered at Macy's and had become popular in department stores all over North America: the import fair. Called "Italia Magnifica," the fair was cosponsored by Howard Hughes's Trans World Airlines and was presented "under the auspices of the Italian Ministry of Trade." In addition to decorating the downtown store for the event, Lasalle's set up specialty shops to showcase imported merchandise specially bought for the fair. An Italian Men's Gift Bar was located on the main floor, and the "Salon Di Roma" on the "Fashion Third" showcased Italian fashion by designers such as "the latest Italian Rage," Patrick de Barentzen. The sixth floor featured an Italian Gift Shop and an Espresso Bar while the eighth-floor Country House restaurant featured Italian specialties such as spaghetti a l'asta, maccheroni grattinati and sparagio con prosciutto.

Lasalle's seventh floor, a portion of which had been converted into use as an auditorium after the earlier eighth-floor room was closed and reconfigured, housed the fair's centerpiece, called "Galleria Italiana." Exhibits in the galleria included a specially commissioned full-size bronze cast of Michelangelo's Pieta (the original was currently on exhibit at the New York World's Fair) and scale models of St. Peter's Basilica in Rome and Venice's Piazza San Marco, both built by "world renowned model-maker Professor Savoia," who was on hand to speak about his work. Elsewhere, visitors to the galleria could inspect precious illuminated manuscripts from ancient monasteries, a model of the new Italian luxury liner *Cristforo Colombo* or gaze at Vatican stamps from the Cardinal Spellman Philatelic Museum.

The Vatican itself was represented by a gift shop of religious and devotional articles, and space was reserved for performances of Italian folk music and dancing sponsored by the International Institute of Toledo.

Lasalle's hundredth birthday in 1965 was celebrated in fairly low-key style, with displays, an antique car parade and an anniversary breakfast for employees. A display of clothing from the time of Lasalle's founding was set up on the main floor, and employees were encouraged to wear period clothing for the event. Speaking of the centennial, store president Yamin told the press: "We believe that the best way to celebrate our 100th year of friendship in Toledo is to be of service to the community and to display faith in the future of our city. Accordingly, we are working daily to be an even better store, to be highly sensitive to the growing sophistication, and to be alert to every new idea and service so that the good reputation we have earned during the past century will reach a new high during the century to come."

The big event of 1965, though, was undoubtedly the follow-up to the previous year's import fair, called "Festival of Britain" and running from November 4 to the thirteenth of that year. Lasalle's pulled out all the stops in conjunction with BOAC (British Overseas Airways Corporation), which had recently inaugurated its sleek Vickers VC10 jets in service from Detroit to London. Alfie Howard, the town crier of Lambeth, was present to announce store events, and as before, the seventh-floor gallery housed most of the exhibits, including replicas of the British crown jewels, a Shakespeare exhibit, the Old London Book Shop and the "Pageant of Britain," a display of authentic ceremonial costumes worn by Queen Elizabeth II and Prince Phillip.

Special shops designed for the festival included a British Food Bar on the main floor, Irish Linen and Scottish Tartan shops on the fifth floor and the Piccadilly Gift Shop on the sixth. England's well-established Marks & Spencer department store (colloquially known as "Marks & Sparks") sold its beautifully crafted "St. Michael" brand knitwear on Lasalle's "Fashion Third." Visitors could ride a real double-decker London bus around the streets of Toledo, and noted British artist Raymond Klee demonstrated his palette-knife technique of painting during the second week of the show.

To add a finishing touch to the event, the Country House restaurant on the eighth floor was transformed into an authentic English Pub. Lasalle's even went so far as to import a real London Bobbie, Constable Robert Folker of Leicester, who strolled the store and greeted customers, "chin strap helmet and all!"

In the fall of 1966, Lasalle's joined with Alitalia, the Italian airline, to present its "Mediterranean Holiday," which it described as "a spectacular bazaar and

Lasalle's "Festival of Britain" was held just after the store's hundredth-anniversary celebrations. *Collection of the author.*

exhibition featuring the arts, crafts and fashions of Italy and Spain. Thrill to the fascinating exhibits symbolizing 1,000 years of Mediterranean history on Lasalle's downtown 7th floor…see exciting imports in storewide shops…meet artisans from Florence, Barcelona, Old Toledo…all flown via Alitalia Airlines."

For the event, the seventh floor was converted into a Mediterranean courtyard, where exhibits, some repeated from the 1964 import fair, were installed. Of note, though, were replicas of masterworks of El Greco, the painter most associated with Toledo, Spain, and demonstrations of the centuries-old art of Damasquino, the art of decorating nonprecious metal jewelry with gold. A Mediterranean book and gift shop filled out the courtyard. Music was provided by guitarists Anita Sheer and Tomas Morales.

On the main floor, a Spanish Galleon Shop sold model ships while a craftsman from Barcelona demonstrated the art of creating them. Nearby, the Toledo Spain Shop sold a variety of items, such as replica antique steel daggers and swords, as well as Spanish treasure chests in which to keep them. Throughout the store, desirable import fashions like Cortefiel men's clothing from Spain and Illaria knits for women from Italy were offered for sale.

In spite of success with the import fairs, the store chose not to continue the event for 1967, relying instead on a storewide fashion advertising campaign promoting the idea that "If It's 'In'…It's In Lasalle's," while also running a fall "Housewares Show and Sale," which featured cooking demonstrations and exhibits and demonstrations on the store's sixth floor. Needless to say, the fall housewares event had been perfected at Macy's in New York as well. Lasalle's continued to emphasize its prowess as a retailer of fine imported merchandise on a regular basis, drawing attention to ads which proclaimed that "Only Lasalle's in Toledo could bring you imports like this."

A second Toledo-area branch store opened at Woodville Mall, southeast of Toledo in Northwood, Ohio. A few days after astronaut and Ohioan Neil Armstrong walked on the moon, Lasalle's opened the store on August 4, 1969, inviting customers to explore a "World of Fashion." Full-page ads listed the many brand names carried by the 107,000-square-foot store, each emphasizing Lasalle's fashion leadership for men, women, children and in the realm of home furnishings. In spite of the smaller size of the store, it even incorporated a restaurant like its earlier predecessor across town. Woodville Mall itself had opened earlier in the year, and though it was the only enclosed mall east of the Maumee River, its area never achieved the growth that was anticipated for it. Lasalle's simple boxlike store, with concrete facing above brick infill at the ground level, was likewise not able to surpass the popularity of the older Westgate store on the more affluent west side of the river.

"Mediterranean Holiday" was Lasalle's final import fair, held in the fall of 1966.
Collection of the author.

Lasalle's Woodville Mall store served suburbs on the east bank of the Maumee River. *Collection of the author.*

Perhaps due to Toledo's size, Lasalle's refrained from opening more branch stores in Toledo until the start of the next decade, though it did expand and renovate the Westgate store to reinforce its market leadership in the face of competition from out-of-town stores like Hudson's and Jacobson's, which, with their attractive facilities, were draining market share from traditional Toledo retailers. In 1980, North Towne Square was built on the site of the former Metcalf Field airport on Alexis Road north of Toledo near the Michigan border.

By this time, Macy's in New York had found success transforming itself into a "West-Side Bloomingdale's" under the leadership of Edward S. Finkelstein, a longtime Macy's executive who had made Macy's of California the most profitable of the company's divisions while the New York flagship became dowdier and decidedly less profitable. Finkelstein was called back to New York to turn the company's biggest division around. He duly imported his chic gourmet-and-housewares concept called "the Cellar" to Macy's basement, and the store, under his leadership, gentrified itself with hip boutiques, trendy restaurants and revamped merchandising that endeared it to young, affluent New Yorkers and tourists alike.

The North Towne Lasalle's was a huge departure for the Toledo company and a clear attempt to remake the Toledo store in the Finkelstein manner. The

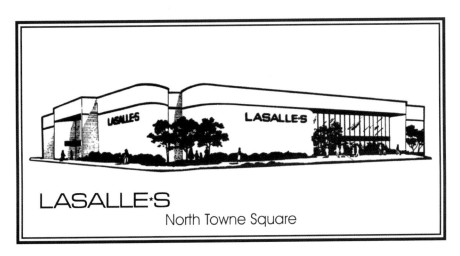

Lasalle's last branch opened in August 1980 at North Towne Square on Alexis Road north of Downtown Toledo. *Collection of the author.*

exterior was attractive in a minimalistic way, composed of rough-textured white masonry with curved corners and deep recesses. Glassy two-story entrances were deeply recessed into the façades and covered by overhangs, resulting in a sophisticated composition of considerable style and allure. Inside, the effect was no less striking, with deep colored plush carpeting, tiled aisles and curves in evidence everywhere, echoing the exterior design. The second-floor Terrace Room overlooked the mall in a series of stepped-down levels more evocative of a sleekly contemporary Las Vegas showroom than a department store restaurant.

Bigger than all the other Lasalle's branches at 162,000 square feet, the new store seemed to point the way to a bright future for the retailer that once called itself Toledo's greatest. Yet Toledo, and its indigenous retailers, had struggled in the 1970s, and the 1980s were to be a decade of change for Lasalle's as well.

Nothing Good Lasts Forever

A s the 1960s approached, the Three *L*s seemed to be at their peaks. Yet the merchants running the stores and civic officials realized that Downtown Toledo stood to lose its hegemony on the retail trade as people sought new homes farther from downtown and other businesses sprung up in order to serve them. Even at this early stage, it was also apparent that the automobile was playing a greater role in the retail world than it had not only in the past but also recently, and the shift was dramatic.

Traffic congestion plagued Toledo, but some of the solutions put forth in the 1950s, in terms of highway development, mainly served to divert traffic from the central business district. Parking, as always, was an increasingly urgent problem. In spite of the construction of sizeable garages, it seemed customers typically preferred the ease of parking in suburban shopping centers to navigating a parking ramp downtown. It simply became easier to patronize shopping centers, though downtown offered much more in terms of the variety of stores and the extra amenities offered.

The era also saw the opening and proliferation of discount stores in American cities. They offered merchandise, often of dubious quality, at extremely low prices. At one time, the fair trade laws developed during the Great Depression protected smaller, independent and local merchants from market erosion by discounters. However, as the discounters proliferated and became national chains, the laws were criticized, lobbied against and repealed. It is interesting to note that this process parallels the decline of North America's great retailers, all such laws having been taken off the books by 1975.

Consumers were thus free to buy anything in a large warehouse-like store and felt they were getting a "bargain" in the process. I overheard, in the midst of the crippling recession that had a stronghold on the nation's economy in the late 1970s, a patron in a Toledo restaurant question the budget discussed for the city's excellent and well-regarded zoological park. "They should just get rid of it," he proclaimed. "Think of all the people they could feed rather than those animals." This narrow approach, which disregarded the value of the zoo that could not be measured in money alone, is kindred to the one often applied to department stores like our Three *L*s. "I can get it cheaper somewhere else," patrons may assume, but few forecast the juggernaut that was coming—the nationwide demise of appreciated retail institutions and the downtowns they called home, with little more regard than a sigh about the capital, the jobs and the contribution to people's lives that these stores represented.

In the late 1950s, while there may have been alarm, there was no understanding about what the future really held for the Three *L*s or Downtown Toledo as a result. Downtown Toledo Associates was formed in 1955 by Toledo retailers as an advocacy group for the central business district. Its activities were varied and wide ranging, including advertising "Downtown Toledo Day" sales, sponsoring special events and proposing a master plan for development of the area. Many of its efforts were successful, and the group stayed together for twenty-three years, until Downtown Toledo was on its last leg as a shopper's paradise.

Somewhat surprisingly, the group's master plan, when it was unveiled in 1959, proposed leveling most of Summit Street and locating an expressway on the banks of the Maumee. The idea that preservation of historic and worthwhile architecture as a route to a city's economic health and cultural well being had not yet taken hold. Ironically, this plan likely led to the ultimate disposition of Summit Street in Toledo.

One of the most compelling of Downtown Toledo Associates' efforts was the installation, albeit temporary, of landscaped pedestrian malls on Madison Avenue and Adams Street in 1959 and 1960. Inspired by the downtown redevelopment plans produced by Austrian émigré architect Victor Gruen, the Toledo body decided to "test the waters" rather than enter into a wholesale banning of traffic on major shopping streets, as was eventually done in Kalamazoo, Minneapolis and, later, other cities as solutions sought to halt the decline of downtowns in general.

Gruen, who had made a name for himself designing the country's first regional shopping centers for Detroit's J.L. Hudson Company and the first all-weather enclosed mall for Dayton's in Minneapolis, later turned his imagination to the plight of the central cities. He proposed how they could redefine themselves in order to compete with the regional shopping centers, which he idealized as a new sort of American town square. His shopping centers, at the time, included a much greater variety of tenants than would be the case today—dime stores, hardware stores, groceries, theaters and restaurants as opposed to the clothing stores that would come to dominate them in later years—and his vision was quite accurate as a result.

Applying the same thinking to downtown, Gruen based his proposed revitalization on two factors. The first was that mall-like promenades and greenery could replace city streets and make the shopping experience more pleasant and attractive to customers. The second involved surrounding the central business district with adequate parking so that cars could only enter its perimeter. His traffic plan sought to alleviate the conflict between cars and pedestrians and convert the central city, for the most part, into a pedestrian zone. His vision could not have foreseen present-day society, which, with great contradiction, seeks health and exercise but is prone to think of walking or climbing stairs as negative and inconvenient.

In most cases, the cities that experimented with Gruen's ideas only embraced the first part; parking was left to piecemeal development and did not come into fruition as envisioned by the architect. As a result, the pedestrian malls attracted interest and traffic when they were a novelty, but more often than not, they were dismal failures that hurt downtown businesses in the long run. Significantly, the blame was placed on the malls themselves, rather than their halfhearted execution, which lacked the supporting parking around their perimeters. Most European cities of Toledo's size have pedestrian zones in their central districts that remain the most popular and best places to promenade, shop, dine and people-watch, and cars are more often than not relegated to the perimeter.

Toledo's malls were installed on two blocks of Adams Street and Madison Avenue between Superior and Huron Streets and were unveiled in August 1959. At the beginning of the experiment, called the "Toledo See-Way," early surveys showed 70 percent of retailers responded that sales had increased due to the installations and 90 percent of shoppers in the area responded positively to the questions they were asked. One week after they opened, the *Toledo Blade* reported that over twenty thousand people visited the malls. As the second week of the experimental green spot began, pedestrians streamed over the colored pavement, through the relaxing areaways on Madison Avenue and Adams Street and crowded around special attractions with as much eagerness as that shown by earlier crowds: "Despite the throngs yesterday, they all still put forth an atmosphere of serenity and relaxation...people walked slowly, stopping briefly to toss coins in pools, to admire flowers, shrubs and picturesque statues, and to window shop."

Comments registered by shoppers at the same time appeared to bode well for the downtown and its enterprising experiment, but one comment was ominously accurate: "This is all very nice, but where does everybody park?"

The malls were originally planned to last for forty-five days, but due to their popularity and a regular stream of out-of-town officials who wanted to inspect them, the project was twice extended, almost to the Christmas season. The next year, the undertaking was repeated, this time only on a three-block stretch of Adams Street. Again, initial response was positive, especially regarding the more elaborate nature of the second installation. Yet when the project ended, negative reactions to the mall were strong enough that the idea went no further. After the novelty wore off, sales dropped, and complaints about rerouted bus lines and the inability of cars and taxis to access the stores directly mounted. Many even questioned the value of the $36,000 expended on the mall, despite the fact that most of it came from Downtown Toledo Associates itself.

More than anything though, critics of the plan reiterated what Victor Gruen knew long before the experiment started—that a lack of inexpensive, well-located and easy-to-use parking caused the endeavor, so promising at its start, to wither and fail. The downtown pedestrian mall idea was permanently adopted in several cities. The *Blade* informed its readers that Kalamazoo, Michigan, got a permanent mall for less than twice the cost of Toledo's temporary ones; years later, after Kalamazoo's downtown had effectively "died" as a retail destination, the mall had to be ripped out, and the same scenario took place in many cities across the country.

Yet all of the Three *L*s continued through the sixties, doing business as before in spite of some disturbing events around them. In 1960, Sears decided to close its Summit Street store in favor of a large new branch in Westgate Village. The closure not only deprived downtown of a major anchor and limited available choices in the area but also took business away from Summit Street, increasing the decline of the thoroughfare that was once at the epicenter of it all and still had historical, albeit rundown, appeal; Downtown Toledo began to limp.

In 1965, the gorgeous Paramount Theater on Adams Street, directly opposite from Lasalle & Koch's, closed its doors after a stint as a "Cinerama" theater. The elaborate old movie palace was too big and too complex for its own good. It was unceremoniously knocked down, robbing Toledo of a sumptuous landmark, once celebrated for its beauty and allure but, in later years, perceived as nothing more than a white elephant. An asphalt parking lot has existed on the site ever since. Though the demolition addressed the parking issue, a gaping hole held sway in the busiest part of a downtown, which was losing its very coherence and appeal, and a major work of art, in terms of the theater itself, was lost forever.

Tiedtke's was the first of Toledo's homegrown stores to bite the dust. In 1961, the respected and well-loved store was bought by Davidson Brothers, the operators of the Detroit area's Federal Department Stores, a mass-market chain store operation, which, at its peak, operated branches as far away as Cleveland. Former president Marvin Kobacker stayed on with the store, but, unsympathetically, Federal's management did all they could to remake Tiedtke's into little more than a Toledo branch of its store.

New management, which came in 1968, presided over the March 1969 opening of a large branch store at the Greenwood Mall on Toledo's north side. What customers found at the "new, new Tiedtke's" was a typical Federal's store, a small deli and cheese counter being the only concession to Tiedtke's former supremacy in the sale and marketing of food products. The branch was understaffed compared to the downtown operation and focused on self-service whereas Tiedtke's longstanding tradition had always promoted the idea of smiling and friendly salespeople as the store's ambassadors. Even Tiedtke's logo was ultimately changed to match the one used by Federal's at the time, whose typeface had been cribbed by Federal's from Marshall Field & Company's long-standing and classic logo.

Management stated at the time that they were "pleased" that Greenwood customers revealed that, if the store hadn't had a sign indicating it, they would not have known that they were in Tiedtke's. When asked about rumors that the store would discontinue its downtown grocery operation as well, store president Douglas Emmons could only say "no comment," a sure sign that it was going to happen. Indeed, when a remodeled downtown Tiedtke's unveiled its new look later that year, groceries were sacrificed to "get more of the retail department store look, rather than the glorified 'Joe's Bargain Store' look of the past." As could have been predicted, the "New, New Tiedtke's" pleased no one.

Just two years later, Tiedtke's abruptly closed its downtown and annex, and within a few months, Federal's filed for bankruptcy protection. By August 30, 1972, it was announced that Tiedtke's would close in three days. Customers rushed to Tiedtke's for one last visit, and employees went about their jobs in a state of shock with an "I-can't-believe-it-really-happened" look on their faces, according to the *Blade*. Marvin Kobacker, who still maintained an office in the store, admitted to the newspaper that he had recommended the sale to Federal's in 1961 because his family disagreed with his proposal to open a large Tiedtke store at Franklin Park and traced the downfall of the retailer to that decision. According to Kobacker, it would have taken Tiedke's all-important grocery business to the suburbs and helped the downtown store remain profitable. He also stated that everything Federal's did took away the original flavor Tiedtke's had, which was responsible for a fatal drop in traffic. "But by that time, I was just another Federal's employee," he lamented, mentioning that the troubles began when Federal's decided to merchandise the store from its McNichols Road headquarters in Detroit and put an end to the days when Tiedtke's knew its customers and bought merchandise to please them.

What happened next was nothing short of calamitous. Cities, particularly "rust belt" ones, were becoming increasingly desperate as they watched their central business districts decay. At the same time, the federal government was offering money to demolish old buildings considered "in the way" of urban renewal schemes. Accordingly, Toledo began clearing Summit Street, which had degenerated into a ghost of its former self, and one of the first to go was Tiedtke's annex in 1974. But the demolition was not without controversy; the works caused damage to Trinity Episcopal Church and its buildings, which were just across the alley from the doomed building.

In May 1975, as the main Tiedtke's building itself was being demolished, a worker noticed what he thought was dust coming from the fourth floor of the once-popular store, which now counted only vandals and squatters as visitors. The conflagration soon developed into one of the most spectacular blazes the city had ever seen. The black smoke that rose from the site drew the curious from as far away as Monroe, Michigan, and police had to work continuously to herd onlookers to safety. At one point, a particularly unruly and mostly youthful crowd tangled with police in a near-riot, characterized by rock-and-bottle throwing, which endangered firefighters who were trying to keep the inferno under control.

Before long, the fire spread to other buildings along Summit Street. If there was anything comical about the event it was the comment of a patron of the nearby Gayety Theater who, when forced to leave the performance of dancer Blaze Starr because of the fire, grumbled, "Sure, just as it was gettin' good!"

The extent of the disaster became apparent after the break of day on May 9, when the destruction was revealed in the light of day. The former store looked "like an abstract sculpture" to one onlooker, and the tall Home Furniture building across the street appeared like a skeleton on its top floors, which were destroyed when the flames leapt across Adams Street. Wind-driven embers caused fires on the roof of the Lion Store's Summit Street building, but store maintenance personnel and firefighters were able to limit the damage at that location.

The rubble was duly cleared, and the Home Furniture building was demolished along with other parts of Summit Street's history. Toledo had changed, forever losing the character it had for many years. Urban renewal promised the open spaces forecast in the 1959 master plan, and Toledo's remaining companies proposed glassy new towers facing the Maumee River.

Over at Lamson's, things were not going well either. After opening two large, glitzy stores in suburban shopping malls, the store found itself with a very heavy debt load as downtown sales dropped at an alarming rate. While the store did close its Maumee branch after the opening of the nearby Parkway Plaza store, it had not felt the need to consolidate before. The Colony Store was the first to go, in 1970, deemed too small and close to the new Franklin Park Mall.

The most devastating bombshell was dropped in April 1974 by Lamson's president Jules Vinnedge, who had succeeded longtime president Fern L. Kettel in 1961. Vinnedge, who was the young boy who ran up to help his grandfather with the groundbreaking on the store in 1928, stated that the downtown store would close in two weeks, citing a disastrous decline in business at the Jefferson Street landmark, but refused to support the claim with actual sales figures. Employees were notified of the closure via the store's PA system, but their ears heard what their hearts had already suspected—that the doors of the store they called home would soon close for good. Vinnedge told the press at the time that he believed Lamson's departure from downtown would not affect urban renewal efforts in Toledo and that the office buildings being proposed "would draw people downtown." Notably, his announcement made no mention of a possible return of Lamson's to a revitalized downtown.

Yet Lamson's problems weren't only located downtown. A few months later, it was announced that the Franklin Park store would be sold to Jacobson's, the Michigan luxury store that sought to gain a foothold in the Toledo market, as its larger Michigan rival Hudson's had already done. Lamson's soldiered on for two years at Southwyck and Parkway Plaza but ultimately filed for bankruptcy protection in April 1976. At the time, Jules Vinnedge explained, "Everyone knows our plight. We're deep in debt." It was also reported that Lamson's had been hoping to sell its downtown store, which was owned by a subsidiary, the Lamson Brothers Building Company, which likely explains one of the reasons for its closing two years earlier.

After five months of proceedings, Schottenstein Stores of Columbus, Ohio, stepped forward as the successor to Lamson's. Schottenstein had built its reputation on the purchase of ailing department stores and selling or converting their properties to its Value City discount format. It proposed doing the latter to the Lamson's store at Parkway Plaza, but an agreement to do the same could not be reached with the owners of Southwyck Mall, who did not want a discount operation of the type that Value City represented in their shopping complex. Lamson's former downtown flagship was excluded from the Schottenstein purchase; it reverted to the holder of its mortgage, the First National Bank of Chicago. It is interesting to note that the elegant 1928 building, which cost almost $3 million to build, was valued at less than $1 million at the time of the bankruptcy settlement in 1976.

Jules Vinnedge, former president of Lamson's and grandson of the store's founder, Julius Lamson, took a position as operations manager for the new discount stores. He couldn't have possibly known of the tragedy that loomed on May 3, 1977. On that date, Jules Vinnedge was shot in the head by Toledo resident Theodore Smith, assisted by his sister Benita. Vinnedge was in the process of taking a cash deposit from the store to the bank when he was robbed by the pair in the Parkway Plaza parking lot. They were apprehended the next day and ultimately sentenced to death, but their sentences were reduced to life in prison when Ohio's capital punishment law was deemed unconstitutional by the United States Supreme Court.

Catherine Towle remembers the Lamson family's reaction to the sad event well. "He wasn't as close to us anymore, but I remember my grandmother and mother being very upset at the news," she relates, and in her daughter Wendy's attic, a clipping file, chock-full of newspaper reports of the thoughtless slaying and its subsequent trial, bears witness to a family's grief. John McCleary, Catherine's cousin, also recalls the event: "That was the moment we realized how low the family had sunk. In the old days, Lamson's would never expose an employee to such danger; armored cars transferred large sums of money. That Julius was subject to it like that was incomprehensible."

The Lamson's building was converted to offices and renamed One Erie Center, but its Jefferson and Erie Street annexes were demolished. It was planned to have retail space on the first floor, but the aisles through which Toledo's

Ghosts of the past—ornate chandeliers, cast-plaster moldings and shiny woodwork—are all that remain to remind visitors to One Lake Erie Center that the building was once a deluxe emporium, Toledo's most fashionable. *Photo by the author.*

most fashionable shoppers once strolled have remained vacant. The building continues to give the impression of a beautifully detailed white elephant.

With Lamson's gone, downtown only had the Adams Street corridor left as a vestige of its former self, though even there, closings and demolitions resulted in parking lots that left the whole ensemble looking like a smile marred by missing teeth. The last two of the Three *L*s carried on intact. The Lion Store suffered a deluge in 1972, when frozen water in the 1912 Adams Street building's fire-sprinkler system burst pipes, showering the floors of the building and causing damage to merchandise and equipment. Repairs were soon made, and the store continued to be a destination for downtown shoppers and office employees until a large new branch of the Lion Store at North Towne Square was ready to open in 1980. The Lion Store announced in 1979 that it would pull out of Downtown Toledo after the New Year. It had, in fact, already vacated its Summit Street annex and moved its famous lions to the St. Clair Street entrance.

The Lion Store's management tried to soften the blow, claiming it would actively seek to build a new store downtown as soon as it could; in fact, a new store with an adjoining office building was proposed for the block that housed Toledo's oldest department store and even pictured in the *Blade* in 1966, but the project was never executed. The store's closing was met by sadness among employees and regular customers, who foretold that a "friendly place," such as the Lion Store had become, would probably not be seen downtown for a long time.

After the closing, the annex building on Summit Street was the first part of the Lion Store to be demolished. All of the historic buildings on either side of it had already been taken for urban renewal, and it sat, lonely and abandoned, for two years after the downtown store closed. Five years after the annex's demolition, the rest of the store was razed. By that time, Toledo was focused on its new waterfront, with its shiny corporate headquarters, open space and its centerpiece, the Portside Festival Marketplace, a suburban-style shopping mall that eschewed anchor stores for a waterfront view. The site of the Lion Store was eventually occupied by the Summit Center office building.

The Lion Store name remained dominant in the Toledo area for quite a few years. The North Towne Square store opened in March 1980 and was initially received well by the Toledo Shopping Public. The Lion Store took on the vacated Lamson space at Southwyck as a home store and remodeled its original store there as well. In 1993, a large, lavishly decorated branch opened in Franklin Park Mall. The announcement of the new store concerned merchants in Westgate Village, who worried that the chain would close the older Lion Store when the new one opened nearby, and they duly filed suit to prevent the move they feared would diminish traffic at the older shopping center. The merchants could part with a collective sigh of relief when Mercantile Stores announced it would remodel and operate the 1957 facility as a home store. Their difficulties proved not to be over though, as the store closed for over four months in 1993 while renovations took place.

The glittering new store at Franklin Park opened in March 1993 and, in its furnishings and merchandise, indicated a youthful and more sophisticated future for the venerable retailer. The Lion Store had a new, updated logo and a slogan that reflected its illustrious history: "A Toledo Tradition for 136 Years." Moreover, the store housed the famous lions on pedestals high above its central cosmetics aisles. When the downtown store closed, the Toledo Zoo had asked for the lions, stating it would keep them until a new downtown Lion Store opened. They made the zoo their home until 1982, when they were relocated to the Southwyck Mall store as a vestige of the Lion Store's history. They stayed there until 1993, when the new Franklin Park store, considered to be a flagship for Mercantile Stores in the Midwest, readied a perch for them.

In 1994, the press speculated about a possible takeover of Mercantile Stores, likely by the May Department Stores Company, which had been acquiring whole chains of department stores for some time. The talks were broken off in 1994, but in 1998, a new suitor appeared: Dillards. The Little Rock, Arkansas–based chain store had grown from a young regional retailer to a national one by acquiring famous names like Stix, Baer & Fuller in St. Louis and Higbee's in Cleveland. When it became apparent that Dillards would acquire most of the names that had operated since 1914 under the Mercantile banner, Toledoans began to ask what would become of the familiar Lion Store name and of the lions themselves.

The company eventually did change the name to fit its corporate format and discontinued events such as the store's popular "midnight madness sales," and it even considered removing the lions in order to sever ties with the store's history. The idea was thwarted only by the cost and effort required to remove each of the half-ton beasts from their perches. The Lion Store's legacy also lives on in many of the store's employees, such as Donna, who proudly identifies herself as "a Lion Store person" and has saved store T-shirts and logo phone cards that she acquired over time in order to preserve a bit of the store's history.

Other Lion Store branches closed, though a few of them did carry the Dillard's nameplate before their demise. With the economic decline of the 1990s and beyond, it became clear that Toledo was overbuilt with malls for a shrinking market; though downtown lost all its status as a retail magnet, it soon became apparent that the Franklin Park Mall and the built-up area around it had emerged as the dominant shopping district of the region. As a result, Southwyck, Woodville and even the newer North Towne Mall began to struggle. They, along with their anchor stores, eventually became

Toledo's famous lions, once city landmarks, sit on perches high above the sales floor of the Franklin Park Mall Dillard's store. *Photo by the author.*

"dead malls" and were closed or, in the case of Southwyck and North Towne Square, demolished.

The illustrious Lasalle & Koch Company met with a similar demise, though it lasted downtown longer than the other two department stores. After the closing of the Lion Store, John Griffin, the president of Lasalle's, went out of his way in a *Toledo Blade* interview to state that Lasalle's was emphatically not leaving downtown and, in fact, was taking steps to improve the store. In reality though, it had been contracting retail space for years and even closed the Country House restaurant, successor to the eighth-floor restaurants so admired when the "Larger Lasalle & Koch Store" opened in 1927.

One month later, a woman was shot and killed in a ladies' lounge in the downtown store in a crime of passion. While it still resulted in a tragic loss of life, as it was not random violence, it should not have had a tremendously negative impact on the struggling store. Years earlier, the murder of an innocent person in the downtown J.L. Hudson Company store in Detroit was widely publicized and negatively impacted downtown sales. It is reasonable to think that the crime in Toledo caused speculation at the time as to whether it was safe to shop downtown.

Technically, the end came for Lasalle's in 1982, when R.H. Macy & Company, flush with the success of the remodeling and rebranding of its stores in New York, combined Lasalle's with its Kansas City division and renamed the Toledo stores as Macy's. Once again, a Toledo store was merchandised from afar, and any connections Macy's might have preserved with the Toledo shopping public were eroded; but John Griffin, now a vice-chairman of the newly renamed Macy's Midwest, stated that the "consolidation of buying, the name change, and other steps will provide customers with better merchandise selections and better prices." Yet the store continued to contract, closing its Tiffin and Sandusky branches in the same year and reducing the downtown store to a mere four floors.

By the end of the next year, Macy's closed the downtown store that had served Toledoans so well since its doors opened in 1917. Along with a general outcry about the store's decision to close, many decried the loss of an amenity that had existed from the beginning: Lasalle's main aisle, which connected with the Spitzer Building arcade to provide an all-weather route from Adams Street to Madison Avenue. At the time of the closing, Victor Tossell, who worked for Lasalle's from 1923 through 1946, revealed that he tried to have the aisle renamed as "Thrifty-First Street," but the idea never caught on with the Lasalle's brass.

Detroit city planning director Diane Edgecomb weighed in on the Toledo Macy's closing, telling the *Blade* that the "loss of a city's last downtown department store is not, in itself devastating" and that "department stores as we know them are fairly obsolete." In fact, the city from which she spoke was the very picture of devastation and obsolescence. Toledo at least had the opening of some new projects, such as the Portside Festival Marketplace on the Maumee River to its credit. However, the little mall was vacant within six years, and some of the splashy though boxlike hotels on the waterfront eventually went down-market or closed altogether in the ensuing decline of the city.

The next year, the Bowling Green store was shuttered, and after that, Macy's completely pulled the plug on Ohio by selling the remaining four stores to the Elder-Beerman Stores Corporation of Dayton, Ohio. Elder-Beerman was in a period of sustained growth and acquisition, but later, in the aftermath of a bankruptcy filing and eventual acquisition by Bon-Ton Stores, Inc., it pulled out of the Toledo market and its former stores in Toledo remain disused.

The disposition of the Macy's building took a tortured course after the store closed, remaining vacant until it was rescued from its dangerously

The great building built by the Lasalle & Koch Company has been converted into use as apartments, but deteriorating metal, temporary placards and an incongruous red door greet pedestrians where countless visitors once flowed in an out of the famous store that made its home at Adams and Huron. *Photo by the author.*

deteriorated state in the late 1990s and converted to apartments. However, its once glamorous first floor remains vacant, unimproved and unused.

With little but the façades remaining of two of the Three *L*s, it is hard to imagine that Downtown Toledo was once a dynamic place that supported such large department stores as well as a vibrant day-and-night community

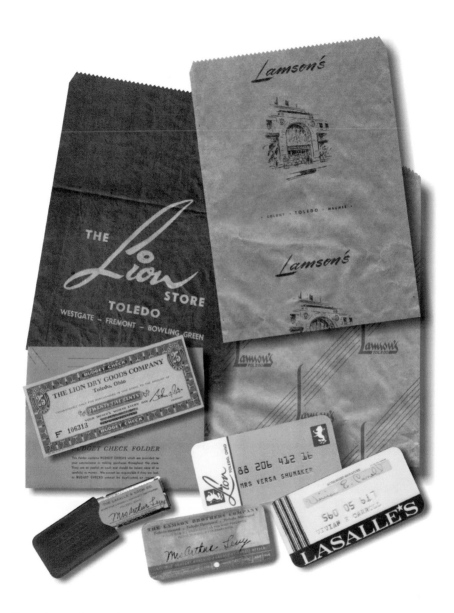

Bags, charge plates and a 1940s Lion Store "Budget Check" are all artifacts of long-gone Toledo shopping. *Bags saved by the late Dorothy Dunsmore Rideout, courtesy of Diane Dunsmore; charge plates courtesy of Scott Nimmo; budget check courtesy of an anonymous Toledo donor.*

that would be the envy of any city today. Sadly, many of those who could remember it in its tremendous upswing are no longer alive, and the impression of Toledo that younger generations may have developed focuses on a city that wrestles with economic and social problems. Granted, a new baseball field, convention center and arena have been built to bring people downtown for events, but a city that has to attract people by holding mass events is a very different thing from a city that attracts them for everyday life, which Toledo so patently was while the Three *L*s were ascendant.

Aesthetically, Toledo's new buildings have not given the city an atmosphere and fabric that improves on what it had in the past. Summit Street, once full of life, remains, in its new garb, unimaginative and mostly devoid of pedestrian traffic. The brutal Key Bank Building, almost unbelievably, presents a massive blank concrete wall to the street, and the space named "Levis Square" is no more than an open lawn such as could be found in any suburb. The most admired building on Summit Street, if not among all of Toledo's buildings, is Fort Industry Square, a whole block of beautifully restored low-rise buildings that colorfully hint at Toledo's lost past.

In conclusion, it's perhaps thoughtful to remember the words of Abbot Justin, who reminisced about his mother's life at Lasalle's and how his own indelible memories keep her life in his mind and heart, ultimately to be enjoyed by readers of this book: "I think it would make my mother proud to know that she would be in some small way a living voice in the history of the department store that played such a great part in not only her work but also her enjoyment."

Well said and well done, good and faithful servant Mrs. Nancy DuVall and the others just like her—whether owner, employee or customer—who played a part in the best times of this remarkable city and its three great department stores.

Sic transit gloria mundi.

Store Locations

The Lamson Brothers Company (Founded 1885)

600 Jefferson Avenue
Toledo, Ohio
Phone CHerry 2-6511
197,800 square feet

Lamson's Maumee (opened May 1943)

318 Conant Street
Maumee, Ohio

Lamson's Colony (opened November 1951)

2128–2136 Central Avenue
Toledo, Ohio
20,000 square feet

Lamson's Parkway Plaza (opened March 1955)

Anthony Wayne Trail and Detroit Avenue
Maumee, Ohio
37,000 square feet

Lamson's Franklin Park Mall (opened July 1971)

Monroe Avenue at Talmadge Street
Toledo, Ohio
90,000 square feet

Lamson's Southwyck (opened August 1972)

Reynolds Road at Glendale Avenue
Toledo, Ohio
82,000 square feet

THE LION STORE (FOUNDED 1857)

329–331 North Summit Street
Toledo, Ohio
Phone CHerry 1-3171
242,600 square feet

The Lion Store Bowling Green (opened May 1944)

145 North Main Street
(Appliance and home furnishings store)
Bowling Green, Ohio

The Lion Store Bowling Green (opened 1945)

110 North Main Street
(Fashion store)
Bowling Green, Ohio

The Lion Store Fremont (opened November 1950)

217–219 Front Street4
Fremont, Ohio

The Lion Store Westgate (opened August 1957)

Central Avenue at Secor Road
Toledo, Ohio
100,000 square feet; expanded to 186,000 square feet

The Lion Store Southwyck (opened August 1972)

Reynolds Road at Glendale Avenue
Toledo, Ohio
190,000 square feet

The Lion Store North Towne Square (opened March 1980)

Alexis Road at Telegraph Road
Toledo, Ohio
162,000 square feet

The Lion Store Franklin Park Mall (opened August 1993)

Monroe Avenue at Talmadge Street
Toledo, Ohio
190,000 square feet

THE LASALLE & KOCH COMPANY [FOUNDED 1865]

513 Adams Street
Toledo, Ohio
Phone CHerry 1-8811
398,000 square feet

Lasalle's Bowling Green (opened January 1945)

139 South Main Street
Bowling Green, Ohio
24,000 square feet

Lasalle's Tiffin (opened August 1947)

71 South Washington Street
Tiffin, Ohio
29,000 square feet

Lasalle's Sandusky (opened November 1949)

Columbus Avenue at Washington Row
Sandusky, Ohio
46,000 square feet

Lasalle's Westgate (opened February 1962)

Central Avenue at Secor Road
Toledo, Ohio
152,000 square feet

Lasalle's Woodville Mall (opened April 1969)

Woodville Road
Northwood, Ohio
107,000 square feet

Lasalle's North Towne Square (opened August 1980)

Alexis Road at Telegraph Road
Toledo, Ohio
162,000 square feet

Appendix B

Store Directories

It is impossible to represent the organization and layout of large department stores such as the Three *L*s because they changed so much over time. Some changes were major; for example, when Lasalle & Koch's added three floors in 1927, the whole layout of the store changed in the process. Likewise, as the Lion Store grew and later remodeled, departments changed location as well. In some cases, the stores developed new names or new lines of merchandise, causing differences as well. The purpose of these directories is to give an idea of the arrangement of these stores in the late 1950s to early 1970s. The reader can consult the document and imagine moving through these large stores, and it is hoped that their inclusion stimulates the memory.

THE LAMSON BROTHERS COMPANY: DOWNTOWN STORE DIRECTORY

Basement

Lamson's Downstairs Budget Store

Main Floor

Accessories•Bakery•"Be Somebody" Shop•Blouses•Books•
Candies•Collegeset Shoes•Cosmetics•Drugs•Fine Jewelry•Gloves•Hair
Piece Center•Handbags•Hat Bar•Hosiery•Housewares•Jefferson
Shop•Jewelry•Luggage•Men's Sportswear•Men's Furnishings•Midtown
Lingerie•Midtown Shoes•Midtown Sportswear•Neckwear•Notions•Photo
Studio•Small Leather Goods•Stationery•Toiletries

Jefferson Avenue Annex

Boys' Wear•Ego-Men-Triks•Men's and Boys' Shoes•Men's
Clothing•Men's Hats

Erie Street Annex

Chevalier Wine Cellar•Customer Service Desk•Patio Room
Restaurant•Special Picture Gallery

Erie Street Mezzanine

Personnel Office

Second Floor

Daytime Dresses•Foundations•Lingerie•Loungewear•Maternity
Fashions•Midtown Coats•Midtown Dresses
Young World of Fashion Children's Shoes•Children's Wear•Girls'
Wear•Hi-Shop•Infants' Furniture•Infants' Wear•Pre-Teen Wear

Fashion Third

Better Coats•Better Dresses•Better Sportswear•Bridal Salon•Canned Ego Salon•Fur Salon•Junior Coats•Junior Dresses•Junior Pit•Junior Sportswear•Millinery Salon•Miss Lamson Shop•Moderate Dresses•Moderate Sportswear•Pappagallo Shop•Shoe Salon•The 101 Room•Town and Country Coats•Wig Salon•Young Ideas Shop•Young Signature Shop

Fourth Floor

Antique Corner•Beauty Salon•Carpeting•Furniture•Home Entertainment Center•Home Planning Center•Lamps•Pictures and Mirrors•Records•Rugs•Sleep Shop•Summer Furniture

Fifth Floor

Art Needlework•Bath Shop•Bedding•China•Curtains•Domestics• Draperies•Executive Offices•Fabrics•General Offices•Gift Shop•Glassware •Linens•Toys•Yarns

The Lion Store: Downtown Store Directory

Lower Floor

China•Clocks•Gifts•Housewares•Silverware•Small Appliances•The Lion Thrift Basement•Toys

Street Floor

Accessories•Books•Budget Lingerie•Candy•Cosmetics•Drugs•Fine Jewelry•Gloves•Gourmet Shop•Handbags•Hat Bar•Hosiery•Jewelry•Men's Clothing•Men's Dress Shirts•Men's Furnishings•Men's Hats•Men's Shoes•Men's Sport Shirts•Men's Sportswear•Neckwear•Notions• Popular Sportswear•Records•Rivets Shop•Slipper Bar•Small Leather Goods•Stationery•Trim the Tree Shop•Umbrellas•Watch Repair•Wig Bar•Young Men's 11th Hour Shop

Street Floor Annex B

Bath Shop•Linens

Street Floor Annex C

Art Goods•Art Needlework•Fashion Fabrics•Luggage•Sewing Machines

Summit Street Annex

Appliance Center•Coral Room Restaurant

Second Floor

Better Dresses•Bridal Shop•Dresses•Fashion Coats•Formal Shop•Fur Salon•Junior Dresses•Junior Fashion Coats•Junior Sportswear•Millinery• Sophisticate Shop•Sportswear•Suits•"77" Shop•"Tempo" Shop•Women's Shoes•Women's World•Young Juniors
Children's World Boys' Shop•Children's Shoes•Girls' Shop•Infants' Furniture•Infants' Shop•Jr. Boys' Shop•Jr. Girls' Shop•Jr. Teens' Shop•Kindergarten

Second Floor Mezzanine

Casual Dresses•Casual Sportswear•Popular Dresses

Third Floor

Draperies•Floor Coverings•Furniture•Lamps•Mirrors•Pictures

Fourth Floor

Employee Cafeteria•Executive Offices•Personnel

Fifth Floor

Advertising•Display Shop

The Lasalle & Koch Company: Downtown Store Directory

Lower Level

Budget Photo Studio•Lasalle's Budget Store•Luncheonette•Shoe Repair

Main Floor

Accessories•Blouses•Books•Candy•Dress Shirts•Fine Jewelry•Flower Shop•Gourmet Foods•Handbags•Hat Bar•Hosiery•Jewelry•Jewelry Repair•Main Floor Sportswear•Men's Accessories•Men's Furnishings•Men's Hats•Men's Shoes•Men's Sportswear•Millinery• Notions•New Traditions•Razor Shop•Scarves•Service Desk•Shoe Spot•Small Leather Goods•Sport Shirts•Stationery•Sweaters•Ties•Young Men's Shop

Mezzanine

Coins and Stamps•Men's Clothing•Men's Outerwear•Repair Center

Second Floor

Beauty Salon•California Shop•Foundations•Junior Intimate
Shops•Loungewear•Miss Lasalle Dresses•Misses' Sleepwear•One Stop
Maternity Shop•Photo Reflex Studio•Robes
Shoe Shops Boulevard Shop•Cobbler's Corner•Designer Shop•Four
Seasons Shop

Third Floor: Fashion Third

After 5 Shop•Beach Shop•Better Blouses•Better Dresses•Better
Sportswear•Better Sweaters•Coats•Coats•Contemporary
Sportswear•Country Corner•Dresses•Fur Salon•Perspective•Sportswear•
Suits•Tannery•The Little Shop•Weather or Not Shop•Women's
World•Young Collector
Junior Scene Junior Coats•Junior Dresses•Junior Sportswear

Fourth Floor

Young World Boys' Wear•Children's Accessories•Children's Shoes•Girl's
Wear•Infants•Luggage•Subteen Charm Court•Teen Shop•Toddlers

Fifth Floor

Art Needlework•Bedspreads•Comforters•Custom Draperies•Domestics•
Draperies•Fabrics•Sheets•Singer Sewing Machine Center

Sixth Floor

China•Cookware•Crystal•Fireplace Shop•Flea Market•Gifts•Glassware•
Housewares•International Coffee Bar•Magicolor Paint Center•Major
Appliances•Mowers•Records•Silver•Stereos and Radios•Sweepers•
Televisions•Utility Buildings

Seventh Floor

Cashier•Credit Office•Customer Services•Executive Offices•Lamps•Ski
Shop•Sporting Goods•Toy World

Eighth Floor

Auditorium•Early American Room•English Room•French Room•Grill
Room (Later Country House)

Ninth Floor

Bedding•Broadloom•Chairs•Colonial Shop•Furniture•Interior Decorating
Shop•Karastan Gallery•Mirrors•Music Center•Pictures•Rugs

Tenth Floor

Advertising•Display Department•Receiving & Marking

Eleventh Floor

Employee Cafeteria•Employees' Lounge Rooms•Training Rooms

Bibliography

Bedmar, José Domingo Delgado. *Toledo Monumental y Turística*. León, Spain: Editorial Everest S.A., 2002.

Ferrin, A.W. "Why The H.B. Claflin Organization Failed." *Moody's Magazine* 17 (July 1914): 339–40.

Ferry, John William. *A History of the Department Store*. New York, NY: Macmillan Company, 1960.

Hendrickson, Robert. *The Grand Emporiums*. Briarcliff Manor, NY: Stein and Day, 1979.

Husman, John, and Sandy Husman, eds. *You Will Do Better in Toledo: From Frogtown to Glass City*. Toledo, OH: *Blade*, 2008.

Killits, John Milton. *Toledo and Lucas County, 1623–1923*. Toledo, OH: S.J. Clarke Publishing Company, 1923.

Longstreth, Richard. *The American Department Store Transformed, 1920–1960*. New Haven, CT: Yale University Press, 2010.

Porter, Tana. *Toledo Profile*. Toledo, OH: Toledo Sesquicentennial Commission, 1987.

Waggoner, Clark. *History of the City of Toledo and Lucas County, Ohio*. New York, NY: Munsell & Company, 1888.

Whitaker, Jan. *The World of Department Stores*. New York, NY: Vendome Press, 2011.

About the Author

Photo by John Daraban.

Bruce Allen Kopytek is an architect and author who has been exploring an interest in history. His first book, *Jacobson's: I Miss It So!*, was named a Michigan Notable Book by the Library of Michigan in 2012. Kopytek and his wife, Carole, live in Shelby Township, Michigan, and together they cook; ballroom dance; look after their cat, Bella; and work on various volunteer efforts at St. Lawrence Parish in Utica, Michigan. One of Kopytek's strongest passions is for travel in the Old World, where he enjoys seeing historic settings and collecting books about the locales he and Carole visit. Kopytek's Toledo connection likely began before he was born, as many relatives on both sides of his family were employed by the Champion Spark Plug Company. The city was a stop on annual family visits to the Lake Erie resort of Cedar Point, and he felt strongly enough about the place to take European relatives on a visit to Toledo to see the art museum and its other attractions. Kopytek spends extra time maintaining a blog entitled the "Department Store Museum," which is visited by thousands of people each day and expresses his passion for the history of our long-gone locally operated department stores.